"The World According to CM
By David Black

This book is dedicated to all of those that lost hours, days, weeks, months or even years of their lives playing this game.

Follow me on Twitter: @cm9798

www.cm9798.co.uk

Follow The Higher Tempo Press on Twitter @thehighertempo

Like The Higher Tempo Press on Facebook: www.facebook.com/thehighertempopress

www.thehighertempopress.com

Foreword

It was one of those lazy days between Christmas & New Year – you know the ones, where every day feels like a Sunday but it was probably a Tuesday or something. Me and some friends sat talking about football (for a change) and Alan Pardew being linked to the Crystal Palace job from our own Newcastle United. Attention suddenly changed to who would be next in the hot seat if Pardew did go.

"Probably Joe Kinnear again," somebody quipped only semi-jokingly. This set a lightbulb off in my head – I had a story about Joe Kinnear!

"I've got a great game of CM9798 going at the minute, Kinnear's just taken the Inter Milan job!" Sadly this was true, I was into 2011 and Kinnear was going from strength to strength. After a couple more anecdotes, I thought out loud: "I'm going to start a blog about CM9798"

Maybe it was the beer talking but a few weeks later I did just that. To my surprise, it caught on pretty quickly. I've dabbled with various pieces of sports writing and although friends have complimented it, I'd be lucky if an article attracted 100 views. This was different though, each post seemed to garner more interest and people from all parts of the world were getting in touch to reminisce about this great game. One such user was Chris Darwen, who you may now know as the fella on the FM16 advert who moves to Spain. Chris was very complimentary of my work from the outset, and as an author of a couple of Championship

Manager books himself, it was a no brainer when he asked me to work on this book with him.

I feel it's only fair I place on record my sincere thanks to Chris for the opportunity, but also to each and every one of the kind folks who have engaged with me on Twitter during the adventure so far – @cm9798 if you want to get in touch (Plug).

I'm also lucky to have a set of friends who have been enormously supportive of my work – many of whom were with me that day in Tynemouth but several more who have promoted my work without me even needing to ask. You know who you are lads, and thanks for all your help.

I'm also fortunate to have an understanding wife, Steph, who has not only put up with me writing about this nearly 20 year old game but went one step further by being the photographer for an impromptu managerial unveiling photoshoot in the Bernabeu during our holiday to Spain this summer. If that isn't love, I don't know what is. Incidentally, if you want to make sense of the Bernabeu anecdote, check out the blog at www.cm9798.co.uk (Plug plug).

I hope you enjoy reading my trip down memory lane as much as I enjoyed writing it. The beauty of CM9798 is that it's still as addictive today as it was 18 years ago, but with the added bonus of certain player developments being hilarious with hindsight. You'll also find my version of a 'live text' for every competitive England game – these were very well received on the blog, so what I'm trying to say is...if you don't like them, it's your own fault for not stopping me sooner.

David Black, November 2015

Setting the Scene

This game may have been released eighteen years ago, but is still fascinates me to this day.

It's important that I set the scene for you first before we dive into the 1997/98 season. Firstly, I'm on a patched version of the game (V2.93 for anybody who asks). I know people often prefer to play with the "out of the box" version of the game, and to be honest I would too, but the advantage of the patch is that the bugs are ironed out and transfers are amended up to about the half way point of the 97/98 season. For example, Newcastle no longer have Tino Asprilla or John Beresford but they do have Andreas Andersson and Gary Speed. The database is largely the same, but with the odd adjustment. When I started writing the 97/98 blog, the player I get asked about the most is Tommy Svindal Larsen. I can only assume he has been downgraded slightly in the patch, as he doesn't even make the cut to be included in the database for the leagues I've loaded. It also allows the maximum contract to be over £50,000 and actually goes to £100,000. I can't tell you how much I wish I'd had the patch as a child for this reason alone!

Of course back in 1997, the internet wasn't quite what it is now. The patch was available online, but was also distributed via a PC magazine. It wasn't something I was aware of until we got the internet and I re-visited the game some years later, but for the most part I played the game unpatched.

Putting the patch aside, the leagues I've chosen to run are England, Scotland & Spain. CM97/98 had nine selectable leagues, the first time in the series more than three leagues had been available and selectable. The series had tested the waters of the European league with two separate releases during the CM2 series where the English league wasn't selectable and you had three Divisions per CD – Spain, Belgium & Holland on one and Italy, France & Germany on the other. This was with the 95/96 season data, and was the first step towards the dozens of leagues available on today's *Football Manager* releases. It's also worth noting that 97/98 was able to run without a CD once it was installed, which was a clever marketing ploy to get as many people playing the game as possible before the release of CM3, which was a giant stride forward for the series in terms of presentation and options.

Back to 1997 though and the Premier League is about to enter its 6th season. Manchester United have been the dominant force since the Premier League was launched for the 92/93 season, winning the title four times, with only Blackburn Rovers managing to break the trend in the 94/95 season. To be very honest, I don't think I've ever had a season on the default database where Manchester United haven't won the League, so they are red hot favourites.
The 1997/98 season is also the first year where the Champions League was expanded to twenty-four teams, with six groups of four rather than the previous setup of sixteen teams. The extra entrants were the runners-up from eight domestic leagues – Germany, England, France, Netherlands, Italy, Portugal, Spain&

Turkey. The runners up enter at the qualifying round stage, whilst the winners go straight into the groups. All of this adds extra spice, as Newcastle United join Manchester United in the Champions League and it means 2nd place is a potentially vital spot with all of the extra income the competition generates. Newcastle should therefore be in a good position to challenge at the top. Kenny Dalglish however, is in the process of dismantling Kevin Keegan's entertainers and purchasing several substandard replacements. To make matters worse, star striker Alan Shearer is injured until the turn of the year after a pre-season game. It was always of great annoyance to me that his injury was hard coded into the game, though I did cheat once as a kid and load the editor and change his name to Al Shearer to get past the injury. Massive rebel, I know.

In the real world, Arsenal did the double in the 1997/98 season as Arsene Wenger announced himself as a force in the English game. They have a good but ageing squad, their big plus in the 1997/98 season was the emergence of Nicolas Anelka. He's loaded with potential in the game but in my experience, rarely reaches it. Overmars, Bergkamp and Wright are a handful though, as well as a very young Patrick Vieira. Emmanuel Petit is a left back/left midfielder, so there is little prospect of the famous Vieira & Petit partnership that made Arsenal so difficult to breakdown. Of course the famous back five are still there.
Liverpool are another side loaded with potential, including a very young Michael Owen. They also have bags of experience, with Paul Ince having signed over the summer. Spice boys Fowler, McManaman,

Redknapp and McAteer are all present, whilst German veteran Karl Heinz Riedle is still very good. There's also a nineteen-year-old Jamie Carragher, but he's a defensive midfielder. Roy Evans tries to keep this lot in check and they're usually pretty good.

Chelsea are going through a phase of player managers. In the default version, Gullit is the boss but he was replaced during the season by player-manager Gianluca Vialli. Due to winning the 96/97 FA Cup, Chelsea play in the now defunct Cup Winners Cup. Thursday nights, Channel 5...On a serious note though, they have the brilliant Gianfranco Zola along with numerous other stars including Di Matteo, Flo, Leboeuf, Vialli himself and Andy Myers. Sorry Andy. They also have a thirty three year old Mark Hughes.

At the other end of the table, Barnsley don't usually last long under Danny Wilson. They'll perform admirably but usually get relegated. Coventry, who have player-manager Gordon Strachan, rely very heavily on Dion Dublin, now of *Homes under the Hammer* fame. He's wanted by several big clubs as the game starts – if they keep hold of him, they'll be fine. If he goes, it's all down to Viorel Moldovan. Nobody wants that. Southampton are in a similar situation with Matthew Le Tissier, who will not be short of offers, whilst Bolton are usually in and around the bottom three as a thirty six year old Peter Beardsley leads the line with Dean Holdsworth. Crystal Palace signed Lombardo & Padovano and this is sometimes enough to keep them up, but they're not the best at the back.

The rest? Villa & Leeds are probably the best of the middle bunch, Villa in particular can spring a surprise with Yorke, Collymore & Southgate amongst their ranks. Leicester have a very highly rated youngster by the name of Emile Heskey, back before he even knew Sven Goran Eriksson and valued at £9m. Blackburn have an ageing but canny squad, Derby have the likes of Baiano & Eranio to keep them out of trouble, Sheff Wed have people's favourite Niclas Alexandersson alongside Carbone & di Canio. West Ham have two players with huge potential in Rio Ferdinand and Trevor Sinclair, but Julian Dicks is deemed a star player so don't get too excited. Wimbledon are coming to the end of their crazy gang days so if they survive season one, they'll be gone by season three at the latest.

That leaves just two teams. Tottenham, who even before the patch were good. After the patch they've signed Jürgen Klinsmann and Nicola Berti, whilst still holding on to Sol Campbell. Add the recently signed Les Ferdinand and David Ginola to the mix, and you've got a very decent line up. Everton are the other remaining team, who look fairly terrible on paper but always perform well depending on what happens with their manager. Howard Kendall is usually poached by Wales, and his replacement determines how they perform. Duncan Ferguson is the man in demand. It'll be interesting to see where he ends up.
Away from England, Scotland is of course centred on the big two, Celtic & Rangers. Celtic are about to enjoy their first season of a love affair with Henrik Larsson, but Rangers have the much stronger side. Brian Laudrup is the real diamond, supported by Paul

Gascoigne, Ally McCoist, Joachim Bjorklund and Marco Negri. They are a force not only in Scotland but potentially in Europe, too.

It's almost similar in Spain, but on a much grander scale. Barcelona, under Louis van Gaal, still have an amazing squad despite the sale of Ronaldo, who they have replaced with Sonny Anderson. In retrospect, they might have picked differently, although I suppose Sonny didn't do too bad if you look at the bigger picture – Barca did, in real life, win the league. Rivaldo, Guardiola, Figo, Luis Enrique; I could go on. The squad is packed with star players. Real Madrid also have a talent-rich squad, including Morientes, Karanka, Mijatovic, Raul, Seedorf and Roberto Carlos. In the 1996/97 season ending tournament *Le Tournoi*, Roberto Carlos shot to prominence with *that* free kick against France, so it should come as no surprise that his set piece & shooting stats are both at twenty. They also have a certain Davor Suker, who would go on to collect the Golden Boot at the World Cup in 1998.

Speaking of the World Cup, that will be my focus throughout this book. I'm going to take charge of England, and try to better our last sixteen finish. I might even take Gazza, which Glenn Hoddle failed to do in real life. There's a "tip" for this game, you can manage any national team of the league's you've loaded if you enter the real managers name as the manager name, so unfortunately I will be doing this in the guise of Glenn Hoddle. Rest assured though, there won't be an Eileen Drewery mention beyond this page. England's World Cup qualification is in the balance as we start the game, but more on that later.

So, if you're still with me, that is the World we are about to enter. Now, won't you join me in a stroll down memory lane?

July

July 16th 1997. It's a date anybody who's played this game will be familiar with. The first day of the new season – fixtures are out, budgets are starting to take shape, and you've probably just sat through the irritant that is every team in the game flashing up in their team colours in an undecipherable order. I've decided, after eighteen years, that this is in order of ability; with the best team first and the very worst team last. Obviously I've had too long down the years to think about that!

The game has finished creating and important dates for your diary are announced - the Charity Shield, the World Club Cup, The European Super Cup, but most importantly for me, England's next fixture, which is a friendly with Scotland on the 20th August. It's in Scotland, so I'm already worried about that. That's very much future Dave's (well, Glenn's) problem though, so we'll worry about that in the next chapter.

Borussia Dortmund came from nowhere to win the 1997 Champions League so they have the honour of playing in the aforementioned cup games. The Charity Shield will see Man Utd take on Chelsea, whilst the Spanish version will be Real Madrid vs Barcelona over two legs. That's some game to open a season with, it's no wonder they do it over two legs.

So we're underway and there's a few vacancies need filling – firstly at Aberdeen, who poach Tommy McLean from Dundee Utd. Bobby Gould is very insecure at Wales, poor bloke. No offence to the fans of the following teams, but the appointments at Greenock

13

Morton, Montrose, Elche and Raith Rovers will not make too much difference to the direction of this season.

Bayern are the first to strengthen their team, obviously sick of being in Borussia Dortmund's shadow for a few months. Stefan Beinlich, an Attacking Midfielder Left & centre, signs for £4.9m, turning down PSV and Betis. Speaking of PSV, former PSV manager and all round great of the game Bobby Robson is appointed at Real Valladolid. Dundee Utd appoint Mark McGhee, meaning Wolves are now in the market for a new manager. Wolves are one of the stronger sides in Division One (old money, no Championship back in the 90s) so it'll be interesting to see whom they appoint. Celtic snap up Stephen Glass from Aberdeen, which might help, but it probably won't.

The big transfer of the month sees Man Utd sign Dion Dublin from Coventry, for £6m. As I suggested in the introductory chapter, Dublin is a hot commodity so I'm not surprised he's moved, but a little surprised at his destination. Dublin turned down Arsenal, Villa, Spurs & Chelsea, which is quite an array of suitors. I didn't really pay Man Utd the attention their squad deserves earlier, so allow me to elaborate. Eric Cantona's surprise retirement left a hole in Man Utd's squad, leading to the signing of Teddy Sheringham from Spurs. They do however have Ole Solskjaer, Andy Cole and Paul Scholes, who is a Forward Centre, essentially meaning they have four very good forwards. So adding Dion Dublin to the mix is probably a bit of overkill, but he can also play centre back so that's an option. Of course, Dion has already played for Man Utd in his career. Fun fact – if you add Cantona in the editor, his player history will load due to his quick removal from the database following his unexpected retirement.

Just when you think things couldn't get any more dramatic, Blackburn spend £4.7m on Nigel Quashie. Nigel is playing for England Under 21s so is earmarked for a bright future – this is long before he suffered several relegations and declared for Scotland. Quashie turned down Sheff Wed, Derby, Wimbledon and Division 2 Fulham. Fulham were another beneficiary of the patch, injected with £8m transfer fund under the guidance of Ray Wilkins.

August
Boom! August kicks off with Kevin Davies signing for Chelsea. Back in these days, Kev was a highly rated youngster at Southampton. Chelsea are stocked with strikers though, so I don't know how much they need him. Still, £3.2m has hardly broken the bank and he's another England Under 21 International.

Sabri Lamouchi joins Juventus from Auxerre. I recently ran a series of votes to decide the best ever XI on CM97/98 and Lamouchi was at least nominated, though he didn't make the final eleven. An attacking midfielder right or centre and French International, £4.1m is a good price. Juve had to fight off Monaco, Marseille, PSG & Parma for his signature. Juve have absolutely no need for him, given their midfield currently includes Zidane, Conte, Di Livio, Deschamps & Davids, but whatever.

15

It's Charity Shield time! Back before we cared for Communities, it was all about the Charity. Man Utd certainly got in the spirit, starting seventeen-year-old Alex Notman alongside Paul Scholes up front, Terry Cooke on the right wing and Wes Brown alongside David May at centre back. Laurent Charvet scores the winner just before half time in a thrill a minute 1-0 win. Ed de Goey takes man of the match so the youngsters obviously tried, at least.

The Spanish version takes places the next day, with the first leg of the Super Copa taking place at the Bernabeu. Josep Guardiola, who you could say has gone on to achieve a modicum of success as a manager, scores a third minute winner setting Barcelona up nicely for the return leg next week. Albert Ferrer is the man of the match, it must have been an awesome display from the right back amongst all the attacking talent.

A series of lower league Scottish sides keep offering me work. Sorry boys 'Glenn' is just not interested. Barcelona decide to sign Robert Pires for £8m, exclusively a left sided midfielder back in 1997. Metz will miss him. Atletico Madrid also bid for Pires, and so did Juventus, who as discussed, just simply don't need him.

Wolves finally make an appointment, poaching Ray Harford (RIP) from West Brom. That'll go down well between two Midlands rivals. As I mentioned earlier, that Wolves squad is full of talent – Dean Richards (also RIP), Dougie Freedman, a sixteen-year-old Robbie

Keane and thirteen times England cap Steve Bull. The game bizarrely claims he has no International goals, even though he actually netted four times for his country. He was part of the 1990 World Cup squad, but it's fair to say I probably won't call him up.

The first day of the season arrives and the big game sees Man Utd win 1-0 at Everton – Dublin with the goal. I've got to have big Dion in the England squad. Derby top the table though after thrashing Bolton 5-1 at Pride Park – Paulo Wanchope getting two. The big surprise is at Oakwell, where Barnsley announce their arrival in the Premier League with a 3-0 win over Blackburn. That'll teach me for saying they had no chance!
Is it that time already!? I need to pick my squad for the Scotland friendly. Shearer is out for a while, Fowler is also out for a month and Scholes has picked up an injury, so teenagers Owen & Heskey are in, as is Dion. Darren Anderton has torn his hamstring and is out for a massive FIVE months. That's not so much a tear as an obliteration. As tempting as it is to call up Burnley player/manager Chris Waddle, I think I'll go for Rob Lee instead. Tony Adams is broken so Gary Pallister is in. I like to play 3-5-2 wingbacks, which was all the rage at the time so the formation seems to be well received.

So in 1997, England are a year on from the high that was Euro 96. This tournament was very much a return to popularity for the England national team, following a terrible Euro 92 and the failure to qualify for the 94 World Cup, all under Graham Taylor. After the high that was Italia 90, things fell apart dramatically. Terry Venables took charge and Euro 96 saw England lose in the Semi Finals on penalties, and Hoddle's appointment was pre-arranged. Because of England's dreary few years and automatic qualification to Euro 96, their coefficient was fairly low and led to them being paired with Italy in the World Cup 98 Qualifying group. Because the game starts three quarters of the way through the campaign, the previous results stand and England are second to Italy, trailing by a point. With only two games to play, including the finale away in Italy, England are guaranteed at least the playoffs, but of course in real life Italy fluffed their lines away in Georgia and England went to Rome only needing a point, which of course they got. I doubt the same opportunity will be afforded to me, but we live in hope.

Barcelona win the Super Copa, completing a 2-0 home win over Real Madrid. De La Pena and Sonny Anderson get the goals and Contreras, Madrid's keeper, gets man of the match, so you know it was a pummelling. Pires is an unused substitute, which he might have to get used to.

The inevitable happens and Wales sack Bobby Gould. In a group containing Holland, Belgium & Turkey, the Welsh have amassed seven points from six games – and when you think the group contains San Marino, it's maybe not hard to see why he has been let go. My money is on Howard Kendall to get the job, but I've once seen it go to Deportivo's manager Carlos Alberto.

More Premier League games, and Blackburn's nightmare continues with a 3-1 home loss to Wimbledon. Barnsley move to the top after a 2-0 win over Bolton. Liverpool and Chelsea play out an entertaining 3-3 draw, Michael Owen celebrating his England call up with two goals. Newcastle don't play as they have their Champions League qualifier, winning the first leg 1-0 against Swiss side Lucerne. Young Jon Dahl Tomasson with the goal. Tomasson obviously went on to have a great career but he never adapted in England, too much too soon I think. One result that catches my eye is Gothenburg 8 – 2 Galatasaray, whilst Barca win 2-1 in Ostrava. Rangers have already won one round, knocking out Dynamo Kiev, and now hold a 3-1 advantage over HJK Helsinki.

West Brom appoint Gordon Milne, who was manager at Turkish side Bursaspor. Why he was there, I have no idea. Speaking of no idea, Wales appoint Bernd Krauss as manager. Any ideas? Well, he was the Real Sociedad manager, and now...he isn't. I've had to research this guy and he went on to manage Borussia Dortmund for two months, then he seems to have been everywhere else. Good luck, Wales.

Rangers sign Heskey for a cool £9.25m, turning down Arsenal in the process. Big move, I'm sure Brian Laudrup has long dreamt of supplying somebody of Heskey's quality. Not satisfied with that, Rangers also spend £4.9m on Dean Richards of Wolves. Richards had the choice of Boro, Sheff Wed & Leeds, but went for the lure of the Champions League. I can't say I blame him.

It's game day for me. I need to inspire confidence in this new era and that will involve not losing in Scotland. It's difficult to pick a team, most of the players have only played a couple of games for their club. I've decided to roll out the bold 3-1-3-3, which involves international debuts for Owen & Heskey. Eighteen- year-old Rio Ferdinand is a sub. Scotland go with a more conventional 4-4-2, pairing Duncan Ferguson and Scott Booth (of Borussia Dortmund, for some reason) up front.

Owen scores on his debut as we mostly dominate first half, Beckham has a second disallowed for offside. Beckham has a pace stat of five, so I was always sceptical when he got in behind the defence. It's more of the same in the second half, but Goram saves a Merson penalty on fifty six minutes and that turns the tide somewhat. Despite some heavy Scotland pressure, we hold on for a 1-0 win and it's a great start to my era. Steve McManaman gets man of the match, helped by his assist for Owen's goal. It wasn't pretty but a win is a win.

Bernd Krauss gets his Wales tenure off to a perfect start by winning 3-0 in Turkey. Wales can't actually qualify, so it's all in vain. He did however deploy Gary Speed as a sweeper, so I'm not sure he's as much of a genius as you might think. There were no qualifying games in our group in this round of fixtures so nothing to report on there. Ireland (or Eire, as they are known) can only draw 0-0 at home to Lithuania, leaving their chances of making the playoffs in the balance. Northern Ireland put up a brave effort at home to Germany but lose 1-0 to a Jürgen Klinsmann seven minutes from time. That mathematically ends the chances of Bryan Hamilton's men qualifying, but it was all but over anyway.

International break over then, and as clubs prepare to return to domestic action, Lazio spend £5.25m on German forward Fredi Bobic. Premier League fans will know Bobic for scoring a hat trick for Bolton in 2002 that helped keep them in the league. On a wider scale, he was part of Germany's winning squad at Euro 96, so a very decent signing. Monaco also splash the cash, opting for Crystal Palace defender Valerien Ismael, for the same price as Bobic oddly enough. Ismael turned down Leicester & Marseille. Ismael starts at Strasbourg on the default database and was a great defender to acquire, so I was genuinely shocked in real life when he turned up at Palace. As a result of this in game transfer, he's technically left Palace before he's joined them, which must give you a real headache if you care for perfect chronology.

A third transfer on the same day! A real big one too. Matthias Sammer leaves Dortmund to join Barcelona for £4.6m, turning down Juventus and Real Madrid in the process. Sammer's about to turn thirty but is one of the best defensive midfielder's on the game, who can also play sweeper. He was actually player of the tournament at Euro 96, so his reputation is very high in the game.

It's time for the weekend, and the big headline is a shock defeat for Tenerife over in La Liga, losing 6-1 to manager-less Real Sociedad. I'm no expert but I'd probably appoint the caretaker gaffer after that result. Inigo Idiakez nets a hat trick, the type of performance that got him a dream move to Derby County some years later. In the Premier League, Arsenal replace Barnsley at the top after winning 6-2 away at West Ham, even though Barnsley get a win themselves at home to Sheff Wed.

Richard Rufus moves to West Ham for £4.1m – disappointing Leeds, Sheff Wed, Coventry & Fulham. If West Ham are going to ship six goals, it's probably a good move to bring in Richard Rufus, who is a very highly rated youngster at Charlton.

The Champions League qualifiers follow, and as we're at the 2nd leg stage these games are worth millions to the clubs involved. Newcastle book their place in the groups with a resounding 5-1 win in Lucerne, whilst Rangers win an entertaining game 3-2 against HJk Helsinki at Ibrox, to give them a 6-3 aggregate win. Barcelona somehow manage to draw 0-0 at home to Banik Ostrava but still go through 2-1.

Now that the qualifiers are done, the groups are drawn. There are six groups, with the winner of each going through along with the best two runners up. Holders and top seeds Dortmund are in with Monaco, Rangers and Ararat, who of course you'll all know are the Armenian champions. Real Madrid and Juventus are drawn together which cuts down the possibility of a replay of the real life final of this season. Leverkusen and Gothenburg make up the numbers in that group. Man Utd have the luminaries of FC Croatia and CSKA Sofia, but also the French giants PSG. Bayern Munich and Barcelona are also paired together – it still astounds me that Barcelona finished bottom of their group in the real world, having never recovered from losing to a Tino Asprilla hat trick and subsequently shipping seven goals over two games to Dynamo Kiev, including a 4-0 home loss. Brondby and Panathinaikos are up against those two. Speaking of Newcastle, they're going double Dutch as they've been drawn with both PSV and Feyenoord, something that is actually impossible but the game cares not for same nation limitations, so tough. Tiligul Tiraspol are also in there, the Moldovan champions an easy choice for no points. That only leaves one other group and it's another double nation disaster, as Porto & Sporting Lisbon face off along with Skonto Riga and Parma – who have a truly ridiculous squad.

Whilst all this Champions League tomfoolery has been going on, there's also a round of domestic game. The shock result graphic tells me of Blackburn 7 – 0 Chelsea, which is a shock by anybody's standards. I was expecting to see red cards and all sorts, but it turns out Blackburn were just awesome and it was 6-0 at half time. Martin Dahlin scores four and Ed De Goey gets rated an eight, so read into that what you will. Arsenal remain top after a win over Everton, whilst Aston Villa are surprisingly bottom. Man Utd are ready to pounce, up in 4th.

Kieron Dyer signs for Coventry for £3.9m. Dyer is a defender/midfielder left or right, even though he went on to make his name in the middle of the park. Dyer did of course make his England debut as a right back, but that was under Kevin Keegan where everybody was an attacker one way or another. Dyer turned down a host of clubs including Sheff Wed, who seem to get knocked back by everybody.

Meanwhile over in Spain, Valencia star Gomez Colomer Fernando breaks his leg and will be out for eight months. He's a very good player who at thirty-one doesn't have many years left at the top, so it's a big blow for him and indeed Spain. It does make me laugh though that the news story ends with "he has been withdrawn from the Spain squad for the friendly with Israel." Well, I would hope so. Sociedad finally appoint somebody, as Lorenzo Serra Ferrer takes the hot seat. Nope, me neither.

As we approach another weekend, Wimbledon delve into the transfer market and sign Sasa Ciric from CSKA Sofia. In reality, Ciric had an unremarkable career, collecting twenty-six caps for Macedonia. In-game though he's a great buy for a team in Wimbledon's position, and at £1.8m he won't break the bank either. Good show.

The final games of the month see Tottenham join Arsenal at the top of the table, beating Blackburn 3-0. Arsenal can only draw 1-1 at Newcastle despite Overmars scoring on his debut. Villa beat Palace to climb off the bottom, with Steve Coppell's men replacing them. A fairly standard day in the Premier League is mimicked in Scotland as both Celtic and Rangers pick up 3-0 wins. We're only in week two in Spain but Betis are the early pace setters, putting five past Deportivo. Real Betis have a real exciting side, built around the brilliant front two of Alfonso and Oli with Fernando (a different one to the chap who broke a leg not long ago) pulling the strings. They usually go up against Chelsea for the Cup Winners Cup, so we'll keep an eye on that.

We reach the end of August and it's time for some manager awards. These are based on "performance points" – an in game calculation based on games won in various competitions, plus extra points for goals scored, that sort of thing. As Kenny Dalglish won a couple of Champions League qualifiers, he's got more points than most and takes the Premier League gong. Van Gaal and Walter Smith take it for Barcelona and Rangers respectively based on similar criteria. To round out the month, I'm invited to pick my squad for the upcoming Moldova qualifier. Robbie Fowler is back so he's in, Paul Ince is out injured though but he doesn't fit into my cavalier approach anyway.

September
September starts with a big money move – Brian Laudrup moves from Rangers to Barcelona for £7.5m. Obviously it's a big move for him and he follows in his brother's footsteps in playing for the Catalans, but I question the decision to go and fight Luis Figo for a place in the team. Then again, maybe it gets boring ripping up the Scottish League every week?

Another midweek, another round of fixtures. Nothing shocking at all as Arsenal win again and Man Utd are now up to second – Dion Dublin is captaining the side, for those wondering. Spurs slip to a draw at Bolton dropping them to 3rd, whilst Blackburn continue their

Jekyll and Hyde existence by beating Liverpool 3-1 to move up to 7th. Betis still top La Liga after three games, Barca and Real Madrid have been pegged back with a couple of draws.

Beckham is out for "a few days" which makes him touch and go for the Moldova match, which actually six days away. I'll just let him recover.

As I mentioned earlier, this game has no sense of loyalty so it's no shock to see Fernando Abelardo move from Barcelona to Real Madrid. It should be, but it isn't. It's a bit of a snip at £4.4m too, for a Spanish International anyway. Betis get in on the act by signing Stefan Effenberg, which is not only something shouted at Henning Berg from the terraces but also a very handy German International midfielder. Effenberg costs £4.2m and moves from Borussia Monchengladbach, turning down Arsenal and Atletico Madrid in the process.

It's time for some qualifiers but again nothing involving our group. Only Ireland and Scotland are in action from the home nations – Scotland beat Bielorussia (Belarus in today's World) 2-0 to move to the top of their group. Sweden and Austria are still in the running and have games in hand though. Austria actually play Bielorussia home and away to finish their campaign, which I thought was strange. The Scots actually went down to ten men and Belarus missed a penalty before Paul Lambert and Scott Booth got them the win. Ireland kept their hopes of a playoff place alive with a nervous 1-0 win Iceland, Niall Quinn with the goal. Romania have already won the group but it's tight between the Irish, Lithuania and Macedonia for that second spot. Brazil beat Zambia 9-0 in a friendly, which I'm sure taught them a lot. Oh and Beckham's recovered with three days to spare.

A glance at the job news page and Dave Bassett is very insecure at Forest. They sit 22nd in Division One, and having only been relegated from the Premier League the previous season, they have a right to be upset. Their star player is Steve Stone, who was in the Euro 96 squad, and worryingly for them he is being courted by Premier League suitors. He'll have to get himself to a Premier League club to have any chance of making my squad.

England vs Moldova – As it happened
Welcome to today's live text and what we hope will be a fairly routine win for England. Moldova are the opponents, who have played five lost five so far – if it's anything other than six losses out of six, something has gone horribly wrong.

Team news is just reaching us from the England camp. Gareth Southgate hasn't recovered in time, and England have opted for a 4-3-1-2. Ian Wright gets the nod ahead of Les Ferdinand, whilst Paul Scholes is picked in the "hole" ahead of Man Utd team mate Teddy Sheringham.

England: Seaman, G Neville, Campbell, Dublin, Le Saux, Beckham, Gascoigne, McManaman, Scholes, Wright, Owen. **Subs:** R Ferdinand, Flowers, Sheringham, Fowler, Merson.

Moldova: Koshelev, Gaidamasciuk, Pogorelov, Caras, Secu, Ivanov, Spiridon, Kosse, Belous, Oprea, Nemeskalo **Subs:** Stroenco, Bocts, Rebeja, Timbur, Cletsjenko

Of course, England will have one eye on the game in Georgia, where Italy will be looking for the win that will mean they just need a point against England in Rome in just over a month.
The teams are on the way out of the tunnel, here come the anthems – then it's game time at Wembley.

KICK OFF – England get us underway. It's a must win for many reasons, primarily pride.

2 minutes – **YELLOW CARD.** Pogorelev goes in the book for a late tackle on David Beckham. Hopefully not a sign of things to come.

5 minutes – Dublin commits a foul and the free kick is spun in to the box. Pogorelev gets a boot on it and it deflects behind for a corner. Fortunately, the corner is terrible and comes to nothing.
12 minutes – Another half chance and again it's for Moldova. This time Nemeskalo blazes well over the bar from the edge of the box.

13 minutes – **YELLOW CARD**. Sol Campbell in the book now for a foul on the edge of the box. Ivanov smashes the free kick goal wards but it's well wide. Wake up England!

17 minutes – Finally a chance for England. McManaman gets space on the right and crosses into the box for Ian Wright, whose first time side foot volley is tipped away by Koshelev. Gascoigne's corner is headed away.

22 minutes – A Moldova corner results in a worryingly free header for Ivanov, but he misses the target again. Moldova are sitting deep in the old "Ultra Defensive" formation, but it's proving very effective.

33 minutes – GOAL FOR ENGLAND! England 1 – 0 Moldova (Ian Wright)

England barely deserve this after an abject opening half hour, but it's a wonderful goal. Ian Wright picks up a loose ball thirty yards from goal, takes a couple of steps forward and unleashes a shot that flies into the corner. It's Wright's eighth International goal and I doubt he'll ever score one better.

39 Minutes – GOAL FOR ENGLAND! England 2 – 0 Moldova (Paul Scholes)

It's still not vintage from England but it's a two-goal cushion. Wright is at the heart of this one, running towards the edge of the box before sliding a ball through for Paul Scholes who beats the keeper with a first time chip. It's two goals in four caps now for Scholes.

HALF TIME – England 2 – 0 Moldova

Far from England's greatest performance, they were downright atrocious at times against very average opposition, but a two goal lead is never something to complain about.

Moldova have actually had four shots on goal to England's three, though they are yet to hit the target. All of England's efforts have caused the goalkeeper problems.

KICK OFF – The second half is underway

48 Minutes – Paul Gascoigne tries to get England moving in the early stages of the second half, lashing a shot at goal from just outside the box. Koshelev is equal to it though and tips it round for a corner.

49 Minutes – Close! Gascoigne whips the corner in and Michael Owen gets his head to it, but it drifts wide. Owen has had a very quiet night.

50 Minutes – Owen fires goal wards again but the keeper saves comfortably. Much better from England this half.

51 Minutes – **PENALTY TO ENGLAND**
It's been a great second half so far for Michael Owen and he's going to have the chance to make it even better. The pint-sized striker gets to a through ball before Koshelev who brings him down. Owen's grabbed the ball – he is taking the penalty!

52 Minutes – **GOAL FOR ENGLAND! England 3 – 0 Moldova (Michael Owen)**
No problem for England's latest wonder kid, sending the 'keeper the wrong way. 3-0.

Moldova respond by bringing on Anatol Timbur for Serghei Belous in a straight swap up front.

57 Minutes – A flurry of chances for England. Michael Owen has a curling effort tipped wide before Ian Wright hits another long ranger just over. All England now.

70 Minutes – **PENALTY TO ENGLAND**

RED CARD – Serghei Secu (Moldova)
McManaman clips a ball to the back post and Ian Wright's touch is sublime, taking it past Serghei Secu. Wright looks certain to score but the big Moldovan pushes him over, rather blatantly, and it's a penalty.

71 Minutes – **Missed Penalty**
This kid really is English. Michael Owen's hasn't put a foot wrong in his career so far but he blasts his penalty over the bar.

76 Minutes – **England Substitution**
Couple of changes for England, with Paul Gascoigne withdrawn for Paul Merson and Robbie Fowler replacing Ian Wright.

80 Minutes – David Beckham is the latest to try his luck but the shots drifts wide. The game is drifting towards the final whistle.

88 Minutes – Paul Scholes is announced as Man of the Match in the stadium, a popular choice.

FULL TIME – England 3 – 0 Moldova
Job done for England, though it took a little bit of time to get going. It's all eyes on the Georgia/Italy game, which is just about to kick off.

Italy scored two second half goals to win in Georgia, meaning I'll have to guide England to all three points in Italy next month to qualify automatically. I'm already preparing for the playoffs. Ireland won in Lithuania to consolidate 2nd spot behind the already qualified Romanians. What are the odds on an Ireland/England playoff? Scotland remain second in Group Four, the meat in a Sweden/Austria sandwich with both sides a point either side of the Scots.

Meanwhile, Scarborough appoint Alan Smith as manager. As a former England striker and future Sky Sports pundit, it looks like quite a coup. It's no such good news for Chelsea, as Gianluca Vialli hands in his resignation just a month into the season. The Blues are 13th with eight points from six games, but the shame of losing 7-0 to Roy Hodgson has obviously got to Vialli and he's left on his own terms.

Who remembers Keith O'Neill? Fans of Norwich City probably do, and that is where we find young Keith in 1997. O'Neill was very highly rated at the time, but sadly his career was hampered by injury and ultimately ended by a degenerative bone disease in 2003. In the game though there are no such worries, outlined by the fact Celtic have just forked out £5.25m for the forward left/centre. O'Neill also turned down Leeds and, surprise surprise, Fulham, who seem to be bidding for everybody in an attempt to escape Division Two.

Things can't get much worse for Norwich. Having just lost Keith O'Neill they now lose their other prize asset of Darren Eadie. They sit bottom of Division One with two points from eight games, so although they are now flush with cash, they're in a mighty hole. Eadie has joined Arsenal for £5.75m, if he gets a game he could be a big part of my England plans. He was a man in demand, turning down offers from Blackburn, Chelsea, Derby& Leeds.

Saturday's here and Arsenal's great form continues with a 4-1 win at Derby. Eadie has a two week injury so didn't participate. Chelsea beat Southampton 2-0 as they begin life after Vialli, whilst Leeds slip into the bottom three with a defeat at home to Manchester United. Paul Scholes missed a penalty in the first half but made up for it with a last minute winner. Heskey's broken a toe meaning he is in a race against time to be for the all-important trip to Italy. Generally when Heskey is in a race, I will back his opponent.

Frank Lampard, future Chelsea legend, has signed for Spurs. That's a career changer. At £3.4m, it's a bit of a steal but you have to forget about everything he went on to achieve in his Premier League career. In reality he's a nineteen-year-old midfielder who will turn out well if given the game time. As of this writing, he has thirty-one career games under his belt.

The Champions League group games are under way. In a fairly unremarkable start Man Utd stumble to a 0-0 draw at home to PSG whilst Newcastle beat Feyenoord 1-0 thanks to John Barnes. Tie of the round sees Real Madrid draw away at Juventus after Filippo Inzaghi cancels out Raul's opener.

Chelsea replace the very bald Gianluca Vialli with the people's perm Kevin Keegan. Sure, the perm doesn't quite carry the same volume it once did but I bet he still likes to play attacking football, something which will suit a team that includes so many good forwards.

Another round of Premier League games and there's a big shock at the Dell as Southampton thrash Tottenham 5-1. There's two each for David Hirst & Egil Ostenstad as well as one for the original Stig – Stig Johansen. Spurs left Lampard on the bench. Arsenal consolidate top spot with a 4-0 win over Barnsley, who are somehow still 4th. Keegan's first game as Chelsea gaffer sees them travel to Old Trafford and despite old KK rolling out a 4-2-4, they are easily beaten 3-0. Leeds climb out of the bottom three after a Jimmy Hasselbaink double helps them to a 3-1 win at Leicester.

A really strange round of midweek fixtures follows this. Firstly, there are three World Cup Qualifiers, one of which is Spain winning 1-0 in Slovakia. That in itself isn't particularly strange, but there's a full round of fixtures in England and...Spain. Barcelona manage to win but Real Madrid lose 2-0 at home to Deportivo. But the real problems come at their neighbours Atletico, robbed of both Molina & Ceballos to their country, meaning Christian Vieri is in goal. For those unaware, Vieri is a world class Italian striker. He isn't much of a goalkeeper and Valladolid are the benefactors, strolling to a 5-0 success. The Premier League games are generally unaffected.

In real life, Denilson became the most expensive footballer in the World when he signed for Real Betis for £21.5m. Granted that was in 1998, but here in September 1997, Athletic Bilbao have shelled out £1.6m to bring him to Spain. That is some price difference. It's transfer deadline day in Spain, so Real Madrid celebrate by signing striker Jorge Cadete from Celta Vigo for £7.5m, as well as left winger Joao Pinto from Benfica. Deportivo sign future Liverpool failure Sean Dundee from Karlsruhe of Germany for £6.25m, then go one better by spending £10m on Manuel Fernandez Victor from Valladolid. Victor scored a hat trick against Christian Vieri, so £10m seems fair. Valencia raid Manchester City for Georgian hero Georgiou Kinkladze but Barcelona save the best for last, shelling out £15.75m for Perez Munoz Alfonso. Alfonso was highly rated at the time as his price tag suggests, having joined Betis after failing to make the grade at Real Madrid. He did get his big move to Barcelona in 2000, but it didn't work out, so it'll be interesting to see if history repeats itself here.

Anyway, as the Spanish Jim White packs his bags for a few months, we're back in domestic action and there's a new leader in the Premier League. Arsenal slip up, drawing 1-1 at home to Leeds, allowing Manchester

United to capitalise with a 2-1 win against bitter rivals Liverpool, Teddy Sheringham at the double. Kevin Keegan gets his first points in the bag, winning 3-1 at Palace. Keegan opts for a much more conservative 5-3-2 attacking with Mark Hughes behind Zola and Flo. The result leaves Palace bottom of the pile, yet to record a win. Over in Spain, Alfonso scores a last minute leveller for Barcelona, salvaging a draw from a home game with Compostela. Real Betis remain top but having lost Alfonso, I'm not sure how much longer that will last.

The UEFA Cup is often overlooked but back in 1997, it isn't the bitter sweet Europa League you see today. For starters, it's played on a Tuesday, and in even better news it's a straight knockout played over two legs. Tie of the round sees Aston Villa and Ajax go toe to toe, and Aston Villa come within 6 minutes of a famous win before Gerald Sibon scores to knock Villa out on away goals after a 6-6 aggregate draw. Dundee Utd knock out Benfica 4-2 on aggregate, the damage being done with a 3-2 win for the Tangerines in Portugal. Having said that, Souness is in charge at Benfica and filled their team with English journeymen, such as Brian Deane and Scott Minto, so I'm already less impressed.

October
That earlier heartbreak for Aston Villa proves too much for John Gregory, who hands in his resignation. Gregory only takes over at Villa in the patch, 'out of the box' players will be used to seeing Brian Little in the hot seat. Meanwhile I'm invited to select my England squad for the big game with Italy, and with Heskey recovered, I have very few changes to make.

36

In the second set of Champions League games, it's double success for the English sides. Manchester United win 3-1 away in Sofia whilst Newcastle limp to a 1-0 win in Moldova against Tiligul Tiraspol. Rangers beat holders Dortmund 1-0 through a Paul Gascoigne goal, whilst Panathinaikos stun Barcelona 1-0 in Greece.

It's time for another domestic weekend and Chelsea have a new hero in Kevin Keegan. His new side thrash London rivals Arsenal 4-0 at Stamford Bridge and the Blues are up to 7th. Man Utd's assault on the title continues with a 3-0 win at Coventry, whilst Blackburn are up to 3rd after defeating Southampton. Over in Spain, a ridiculous game ends Real Betis 3 – 4 Barcelona – Alfonso scoring twice against his old club as Barcelona claim top spot.

It's one thing too many for Mike Walker, who quits Norwich. Ironically, they had just recorded their first win of the season at home to Man City, but they don't call him Mike Walker for nothing. The big story comes north of the border though, where Wim Jansen resigns from Celtic. He leaves Celtic 4th in the Scottish Premier League after eight games, six points adrift of Rangers who also have a game in hand. It's still fairly early to throw the towel in though!

There's bad news with just two days to go to the Italy game, as Rio Ferdinand gets injured in training and will miss the game. It's apparently too late to replace him with another player, high speed transport apparently not being invented yet. Villa appoint John Toshack, who was managing Besiktas for reasons best known to himself. Another Premier League club will need a new manager though, as Celtic appoint George Graham from Leeds. Whatever keeps them happy.

The day is here though, the vital World Cup Qualifiers between Italy and England. To re-iterate, the draw England got in real life will not help me here, I need to win, or it's the playoffs.

Italy vs England – As it happened
Ciao from Italy! We're here to cover this vital World Cup 1998 Qualifier between Italy and England. Cesare Maldini's men will qualify with a draw, whilst England need to win to secure their place at the sport's show piece event in June next year. It's the first time the World Cup has included thirty-two teams, so both teams will be desperate to be there!

Of course, the prize for second place is a two-legged play off, so it's not the end of the line for either team tonight – but try telling that to the players in the dressing room.

Team News
Italy play an attractive 4-3-3 and have the usual glut of talent on show. They are unchanged from their win over Georgia last month:

Italy: Pagliuca, Benarrivo, Maldini (c), Costacurta, Apolloni, Albertini, Di Matteo, D Baggio, Zola, Chisea,

Del Piero. **Subs:** Crippa, Conte, R Baggio, Amoruso, Peruzzi.

England were dealt a blow with young defender Rio Ferdinand ruled out on Thursday. There's also a surprise start for Ian Walker in goal, with fears over David Seaman's form costing him his spot in the starting XI. It's a switch to 5-3-2 to try and counteract the 4-3-3 adopted by the Italians.

England: Walker, G Neville, Le Saux, Campbell, Dublin (c), Southgate, Gascoigne, Beckham, Scholes, Fowler, Owen. **Subs:** Keown, Seaman, McManaman, Sheringham, I Wright

When these two sides met last year, the Italians ran out 1-0 winners at Wembley. England had many injuries but there was no excuse to play Matt Le Tissier. Something is different about Glenn Hoddle since then though...

The teams make their way out on to the Stadio Olimpico pitch and line up for the anthems. This is going to be a battle. Are England going to be strong? Have they grown?
KICK OFF - With the anthems sung, the ball is on the centre spot and England get us under way.

2 Minutes – **GOAL FOR ITALY! Italy 1 – 0 England (Alessandro del Piero)**
Oh, England. What are you doing here? Zola has the ball and England decide to push up but get it all wrong, leaving Del Piero one on one with Ian Walker. It's

barely a contest and Italy have the early lead. Disaster for England.

7 Minutes – **YELLOW CARD**. Dino Baggio goes into the book for Italy after a late tackle on Sol Campbell. England yet to really settle.

14 minutes – **YELLOW CARD.** This is a horrible tackle. Paul Gascoigne gets away from Luigi Apolloni who responds by going in dangerously on the Rangers man. Yellow card is the verdict.

19 Minutes – A sort of shot from England! Le Saux hoists a hopeful free kick into the box and it's young Gary Neville who gets a head to it, but it loops harmlessly wide.

25 Minutes – GOAL FOR ITALY! Italy 2 – 0 England (Demetrio Albertini)

Remember the first goal? Well, this is basically the same. Zola picks it up, slips Albertini in who slides it past Ian Walker for 2-0. Game over? Probably.
29 Minutes – Gascoigne tries a speculative shot but it drifts wide. England need something before half time.

36 Minutes – Nearly three! Del Piero turns provider this time, floating a ball to the back post. Enrico Chiesa wants it more than anybody else and throws himself full length, connecting with the ball but it goes just wide. That would have been it.

39 Minutes – GOAL FOR ENGLAND! Italy 2 – 1 England (Paolo Maldini Own goal)

Well, this came out of nowhere. Italy are playing the ball around casually until Luigi Apolloni miss-controls the ball and Michael Owen sets off after him. Paolo Maldini arrives on the scene to help out and lashes a left boot at the ball, only for it to be sliced horribly over Pagliuca and into the goal. England haven't created it but they'll certainly take it.Paolo Maldini is of course the manager's son and captain. That one will take some explaining over the dinner table

42 Minutes – **Yellow Card**. Del Piero goes into the referee's notebook for a handball

44 Minutes – **Yellow Card.** Italy's fourth yellow card is for Alessandro Costacurta after a needless foul on Robbie Fowler. Very scrappy end to the half.

HALF TIME – Italy 2 – 1 England

It could have been a lot worse for England but that late lifeline will need to be built on in the second half.

To be fair, England have grown into the game and have shaded possession, although they haven't actually had a shot on target, which is remarkable really when they have a goal to show for it.

Italy gave away thirteen free kicks in the first half, more than twice the amount England gave away. It's definitely been a tactic of the Italians to try and disrupt England's game.

KICK OFF – Italy get the second half underway.

46 Minutes – Wake up Dion! Gianfranco Zola picks Dion Dublin's pocket and rifles a shot towards goal but Gareth Southgate gets across to block at the expense of a corner. It's sloppy from the captain to be caught by a man about half his size. Costacurta heads the resulting corner wide.

49 Minutes – David Beckham! Great piece of skill to shimmy away from the defender but he rifles his shot over the bar.

58 Minutes – **SUBSTITUTION**
It's a double change for England, with Owen & Scholes replaced by Sheringham and McManaman. Italy had just been taking back the ascendancy so it's a bit more of a midfield three now with McManaman joining Gascoigne and Beckham.
64 Minutes – Enrico Chiesa takes aim but drills his shot well wide. Another goal for Italy now would kill the game.

70 Minutes – **Yellow Card**. Teddy Sheringham clatters into Costacurta and that's a yellow card.

72 Minutes – England have put Dion Dublin up front with Sheringham and Fowler. Time to go direct?

76 Minutes – **SUBSTITUTION**
Italy react to England's changes by taking off a striker for a midfielder. Chiesa off, Crippa on.

79 Minutes – Sheringham does well to roll the ball into Fowler but his shot is gathered by Pagliuca. Shot on target!

83 Minutes – **SUBSTITUTION**
Ian Wright is on for Dion Dublin in a last throw of the dice for England.

86 Minutes – The Italian half has ten blue shirts in it and a goalkeeper. There's no way through for England.

90 Minutes – Sol Campbell is announced as man of the match, whilst the attendance is 82,215. There is nothing else going on.

FULL TIME – Italy 2 – 1 England.
It's the playoffs for England. Italy are on their way to France 1998.

If you think that's bad for England, Scotland go one better by drawing at home to Latvia and missing out on even the playoffs. Republic of Ireland lose 3-0 at home to Romania and only just claim their playoff place ahead of Lithuania. Typically, England draw Ireland in the playoffs and they'll go at it over two legs, with the first leg at Wembley on November 1st.

Norwich appoint Dave Bassett, which is odd considering they are 14th and were in the Premier League last year. I suppose that could be considered a good move by the Canaries. Arsenal go back in time and sign John Hartson for £8m from West Ham. Some of you may be young enough to remember Hartson was at

Arsenal until 1997 before leaving to keep West Ham up. Hartson had other offers, turning down Blackburn, Rangers and Chelsea.

There's another round of midweek games – I don't remember there being this many midweek games ever, but I digress – Arsenal and Spurs play out a 0-0 draw yet leave Hartson as an unused sub. In fact seven of the ten games finish 1-0, six of which were to the home side. Only one game sees both teams score, and that is Liverpool drawing away at bottom club Palace. Man Utd stay top after 1-0 win over Blackburn. In Spain, Alfonso continues to make an impact, scoring the only goal as Barcelona win away at Atletico Madrid. In Scotland, there's only one game as Rangers play their game in hand, drawing 3-3 at Hibs.

Saturday comes without further incident, but it's a much different story with goals galore. Game of the day sees Liverpool beat Arsenal 4-2, who else but Paul Ince netting a hat trick. Arsenal actually led 1-0 at half time but it soon collapsed, even though substitute John Hartson came on to reduce the arrears to 3-2 at one point. There's another cracker, this time at Stamford Bridge, with Chelsea running out 3-2 winners over Keegan's former club Newcastle – Tore Andre Flo with the late winner. Man Utd win again, this time at Bolton – that's twelve out of twelve wins and a nine-point cushion already, with a game in hand. Hate to say I told you so! Celtic draw 0-0 at home to Dundee Utd to slip to 5th, Rangers opening up a four point cushion over the Tangerines after their win at Kilmarnock. In Spain, the Madrid derby finishes 1-1 whilst Barcelona thrash

Valladolid 4-1. The Catalans retain a two-point lead over Deportivo.

Leeds United appoint Victor Fernandez as their manager. George Graham left for Celtic what feels like eons ago, and their search for a new manager has led them to the man who led Real Zaragoza to the Cup Winners Cup (Nayim from the half way line and all that) in 1995. When you put it like that, it's not a bad appointment. Nottingham Forest meanwhile appoint Tommy Burns (RIP), whose previous job would have been Celtic, where he left in 1997.

It's time to name the squad for the Ireland game and I've recalled Paul Ince, not just because of his hat trick but because I'm hoping he and Roy Keane will fight each other and leave the rest to play football. Darren Eadie and Tony Adams are also in, Robert Lee and Gary Pallister making way. I'd rather the first leg was away from home, but hopefully it won't matter.

The third Champions League match day is here and there's a shock result as Gothenburg beat Real Madrid 1-0 in the Bernabeu. There's double delight for the English sides again, Man Utd thrashing FC Croatia and Newcastle winning 1-0 away at PSV thanks to a David Batty goal. Barcelona draw 0-0 at Bayern Munich in a massive disappointment for neutrals everywhere, whilst Monaco beat Rangers 2-0. Remarkably, Newcastle are the only side to have won all three games – Kenny Dalglish's cautious approach paying off with three 1-0 wins.

The weekend comes around again and it's apparently a shock result that Newcastle lose 3-1 at home to Tottenham. Bearing in mind Dalglish has taken to pairing John Barnes with Andreas Andersson up front, I'd say it's a shock they scored as many as one. The Merseyside derby ends 1-1 at Goodison, Danny Cadamarteri climbing off the bench to snatch a point. Arsenal beat Coventry to stay second whilst Man Utd make it thirteen out of thirteen with an easy win over Sheffield Wednesday. It's as you were in Spain and Scotland with Barcelona, Real Madrid, Rangers& Celtic all winning. Celtic are still 5th though.

Burnley have sacked Chris Waddle. As he was player manager he's now available on a free transfer. At least he can now focus on his England recall. It's also time for the league cup 3rd round, and there's some big all Premier League ties. Leeds are knocked out on penalties by 9 man Liverpool after a 2-2 draw. Liverpool were 2-0 down but got back to 2-2 before Kvarme and Matteo saw red – Hopkin missing the penalty resulting from Hopkin's foul. The Scot then missed his penalty in the shootout too so he'll be popular. Chelsea and Blackburn also played out an entertaining 2-2 draw with Rovers going through on penalties. The only shock of the round sees First Division Wolves knock out West Ham at Molineux thanks to an 87th minute winner from Simon Osborn.

The Scottish Coca-Cola Cup final is set and to the surprise of nobody it's Celtic vs Rangers. It's a no nonsense trophy as shown by the fact the final is already set up before the calendar has changed to

November. Still, it's another Old Firm game. My mood is soured by Dion Dublin picking up a back strain, so he'll miss the Ireland first leg at least.

October ends with the usual monthly awards – Alex Ferguson getting the Premier League gong after winning all his games. George Graham gets it in Scotland, presumably for being better than Wim Jansen, whilst Claudio Ranieri, the little tinker, gets in in Spain. Ranieri is currently at Valencia but went on to manage Chelsea in real life, and won the football lottery by being in charge when Roman Abramovich took over. He did however use some of the money to buy Glen Johnson.

November
Well the day is here, England vs Ireland in the World Cup 98 Qualifier. The first leg is at Wembley, we could do with getting a healthy lead if possible but it'll probably be a tight affair.

England vs Ireland – As it happened
The last time these two sides met, there was a riot. Let's try and avoid that today eh?

Here at Wembley, there are some nervous faces around as England welcome Ireland for this World Cup Qualifying playoff. Both sides came 2nd in their groups to Italy and Romania respectively, but only one will get the chance to redeem themselves.

Team News

England recall David Seaman in goal and stick with a 3-5-2 formation.

England: Seaman, G Neville, Le Saux, Adams (c), Campbell, R Ferdinand, Beckham, Gascoigne, McManaman, Scholes, Fowler. **Subs:** Southgate, Walker, Eadie, Sheringham, Owen.

Ireland have come to defend and play five across the back in front of captain Shay Given.

Ireland: Given (c), G Kelly, Babb, Daish, Breen, Staunton, Keane, Townsend, Phelan, Kennedy, Quinn. **Subs:** Moore, A Kelly, Duff, Cascarino, Connolly

The anthems are almost over so strap yourselves in, this could be feisty.

KICK OFF – England get us underway.

1 Minute – Fast start by England, with Le Saux getting a cross over from the left and Scholes heading towards goal but it's blocked by Staunton for a corner. Beckham's corner is poor however.

4 Minutes – Scholes turns provider this time, feeding David Beckham but his shot is well saved by Shay Given.

6 Minutes – **YELLOW CARD.** Beckham fouls Gary Kelly and earns himself a caution. He was a little late on the fullback.

11 Minutes – Chance for Gascoigne this time as he arrives late in the box to get on the end of Beckham's cross, but he can't hit the target.

13 Minutes – Huge controversy here! Scholes is in behind for England but goes to ground after being pulled back by Terry Phelan. The referee gives nothing, not even a free kick.

17 Minutes – Amidst the jeers at Wembley, Phil Babb heads a corner over the bar. First threat from Ireland.

24 Minutes – Scholes is again the architect, but Robbie Fowler can only toe poke his shot wide. England could do with a goal, it's very jittery out there.

31 Minutes – Fowler takes aim from fully thirty yards but it is straight at Shay Given. Well hit though.

38 Minutes – Ireland have retreated deep into their own half – they will not let England anywhere near their goal.

44 Minutes – GOAL FOR ENGLAND!England 1 – 0 Ireland (Paul Gascoigne)

Breakthrough at last for England! Beckham slides the ball across goal for Robbie Fowler, who brings a great save out of Shay Given. Paul Gascoigne is first to the rebound though and blasts the ball home before being mobbed by his team mates. Relief for England!

Half time – England 1 – 0 Ireland

What a difference a goal makes! England were just running out of ideas before Gascoigne struck, and it was badly needed. England haven't forgotten about the Terry Phelan incident though and captain Tony Adams speaks to the referee on the way down the tunnel.

It's been all England for the most part, managing seven shots at Given's goal. The Irish have only mustered one attempt, and that was Phil Babb's header. Surely they will come out of their shells a bit more now they need the away goal?

KICK OFF – Ireland get the second half underway.

50 Minutes – **YELLOW CARD.** Sol Campbell goes into the book after a rash challenge on Steve Staunton. Very silly, Sol.

52 Minutes – Wake up, Rio! Young Rio Ferdinand is caught in possession but Quinn can only blast over the bar. A let off for England.

54 Minutes – **YELLOW CARD.** Gary Kelly is cautioned for a deliberate handball after giving the ball away. Le Saux swings the resulting free kick over but Adams can only help the ball on and out for a goal kick.

56 Minutes – **YELLOW CARD.** Tony Adams is the latest to have his name taken for a clumsy foul on Gary Breen. The free kick results in another Niall Quinn shot but again the big man is off target.

65 Minutes – We've gone nine minutes without a booking – or any action.

68 Minutes – **SUBSTITUTION**
England send on Michael Owen for Paul Scholes to try and liven things up. England will definitely want a second goal.

71 Minutes – Beckham tries a trademark long range effort but it drifts harmlessly wide.

76 Minutes – As we enter the last fifteen minutes Ireland are definitely going for it a bit more. No substitutions but definitely a more attacking formation.

79 Minutes – Chance for Ireland! Kelly crosses and Quinn leaps highest as usual, but again the header is off target.

81 Minutes – Owen to seal it...denied by Given! Liam Daish gets it all wrong and misjudges a long ball, leaving Michael Owen clear of the defence with just the goalkeeper to beat. Given stands tall though and does well to palm the ball away as Owen tries to round him. Still game on.

87 Minutes – Will either side dare go for it in the closing minutes? 1-0 is not convincing but England will be happy to not concede an away goal.

FULL TIME – England 1 – 0 Ireland

Paul Gascoigne's goal separates the two sides but it's a frustrating day for England. The two sides will meet again in Ireland in two weeks to do it all again.

There are no Premier League games due to the England international but with Scotland out and Spain already through, there's action in our other running leagues. Not much of it north of the border though as Celtic and Rangers both draw their games 0-0. In Spain, Athletic Bilbao somehow lose 6-1 at Real Sociedad whilst Barcelona remain top after edging to a 1-0 win over Racing Santander.

West Ham sign Thomas Helveg for £3.2m from Udinese. Helveg was always a very good full back and actually found his way to the Premier League with Norwich in 2004. Danes and Scandinavians in general do very well in this game, there's a number of gems from that part of the world.

This midweek sees another round of European games, beginning with the second legs of the UEFA Cup third round. Dundee Utd get an eye catching 3-1 win over Ajax, but having lost the away leg 4-0 they go out gallant losers. Liverpool, Arsenal, Leicester and Celtic ease through, but Atletico Madrid are beaten by Auxerre of France. Steve Marlet and Antoine Sibierski are amongst the scorers, both of whom would make their way to England in future years with varying degrees of success.

Newcastle's 100% record continues, a 2-0 win in Feyenoord puts them on the brink of qualification –

even if they lose their remaining two games, they would surely be in the box seat as a best runner up if they were to be overhauled. Barcelona labour to a 0-0 draw away at Brondby, a fictional goalkeeper keeping out eighteen attempts and getting man of the match. The result actually leaves Barcelona 3rd behind Panathinaikos and Bayern Munich, who also drew 0-0. Man Utd take charge of their group after a 1-0 win in Paris. Rangers were actually doing quite well in their group containing Dortmund & Monaco but a 1-1 draw at home to Armenia's Ararat checks their progress.

My eyes nearly pop out of my head as Middlesbrough sign Andrily Shevchenko from Dinamo Kiev. Is it the great man who went on to play for Milan & Chelsea? Well, for £3.2m he could even be a decent impersonator and you've got value for money. Obviously the spelling of the surname is missing an 'h' but I can't find any record of a Shevchenko, so I'm going to believe it's him. Boro are going well in Division One, but they are third behind Sunderland and Manchester City.

Savo Milosevic scores a twenty-one minute hat-trick as Villa beat Liverpool 4-2, earning themselves the 'Shock result' news story. Ian Taylor & Rob Jones are also on the score sheet in an entertaining game. The big shock is at Old Trafford though where Manchester United can only draw 0-0 against West Ham. The indignity of it all. Gary Pallister got a perfect ten rating though, so read into that what you will. In a day of shocks, Efan Ekoku smashes a hat trick as Wimbledon beat Leeds 4-0, dropping Leeds into the bottom three. Arsenal keep up the pressure on Man Utd by beating Bolton 3-0, whilst

Keegan's Chelsea smash in five at Oakwell. Celtic can only draw 0-0 at Dunfermline, leaving them in 5th. Bring back Wim Jansen. It's the El Clasico in Spain which is not only a huge rivalry, they're also 1st and 2nd in the table. Real Madrid win 2-1 in the Bernabeu to take top spot and bragging rights.

Chris Waddle is back in the game! Where do you go after being sacked by Burnley? The obvious answer is player-manager a t St Johnstone. He's still got time to earn himself a spot in my World Cup squad...if I get there. Speaking of which, Dion Dublin is over his back strain and it's time to travel to Ireland.

Ireland vs. England – As it happened
Welcome to judgment day – the Terminator isn't quite gunning for England but he may well be for Glenn Hoddle if England don't get through this today. Two weeks ago, England managed a 1-0 win at Wembley over a dogged Ireland side that very much came for the draw. They didn't get it, but a 1-0 loss is not a disaster and it leaves this match beautifully poised.

Team News
Ireland ring the changes to move to a more attacking formation, with eighteen-year-old Damien Duff given a surprise starts on the left in a 4-4-2. Tony Cascarino, playing at Nancy in France, partners Niall Quinn up front. Fellow veteran Ray Houghton, of Reading and also thirty five years old, starts on the right.

Ireland: Given (c), G Kelly, Staunton, Daish, Babb, Townsend, Keane, Houghton, Duff, Cascarino, Quinn. **Subs:** A Kelly, Cunningham, Goodman, Moore, Harte

England are without the suspended Sol Campbell, but Dion Dublin returns from injury to replace him. Otherwise though, England are unchanged.

England: Seaman, G Neville, Le Saux, Ferdinand, Adams (c), Dublin, McManaman, Gascoigne, Beckham, Scholes, Fowler. **Subs:** Walker, Owen, Eadie, Southgate, Sheringham.

The game is being played at Dalymount Park today, for some reason, but the players are out for the anthems and kick off will follow shortly.

KICK OFF – England get us underway.

2 Minutes – Early chance for England as Beckham's corner is met by Rio Ferdinand but he can't direct his header on target.

4 Minutes – **GOAL FOR ENGLAND! Ireland 0 – 1 England (Paul Scholes)**
England have started at a rapid pace and Ireland cannot cope. Robbie Fowler takes aim from the edge of the box, Given gets a hand to it but can't hold on and Paul Scholes arrives to smash into the empty net. The away end is going crazy, the home fans silenced. 2-0 now on aggregate.

6 Minutes – GOAL FOR ENGLAND! Ireland 0 – 2 England (Gary Neville)
Pandemonium. Paul Scholes hits a speculative shot which Shay Given needs to tip round for a corner. Paul Gascoigne whips the corner over and Gary Neville arrives unmarked to make it 2-0. Game over?

11 Minutes – YELLOW CARDS. Ireland can't get near England as shown when Roy Keane arrives late on Paul Gascoigne to earn himself a yellow card. About fifteen seconds later, Tony Cascarino needlessly shoves Tony Adams into the hoardings to earn himself a place in the referee's notebook.

14 Minutes – Nearly three for England as Fowler drives a shot wide. One way traffic.

20 Minutes – The game has hit a lull now, England keeping the ball and not letting the Irish get even a sniff of getting back into this.

30 Minutes – SUBSTITUTION
The Ireland bench have seen enough, Damien Duff is withdrawn for Wimbledon forward Jon Goodman. A change of shape for Ireland.

33 minutes – Chance! Steve McManaman gives the ball away sloppily and Niall Quinn smashes it goal wards. David Seaman is equal to it though, palming it round for a corner. The corner comes to nothing though.

40 Minutes – England's early goals have killed this game for the neutral, but England won't care.

HALF TIME – Ireland 0 – 2 England (0-3 on aggregate)
A very one sided game of football but England will be delighted. It's no wonder Ireland played so conservatively in the first leg. England have managed seven shots to Ireland's one, and Ireland need to score four to go through.

KICK OFF – Ireland get us underway in the second half.

46 Minutes – Gascoigne to Fowler – tipped wide. Neville heads corner wide.

48 Minutes – Neville booked for foul on Babb.

50 Minutes – **GOAL FOR ENGLAND! Ireland 0 – 3 England (David Beckham)**
What a goal! David Beckham likes a spectacular goal, and whilst it's not from the half way line, this is pretty special. Beckham gets the ball 30 yards from goal and curls a shot at goal with what the kids call 'swazz' – Shay Given doesn't even move and the ball is in the postage stamp. This boy will go far.

54 Minutes – Another Gascoigne corner, another chance. This time Paul Scholes heads narrowly over.

56 Minutes – Chance for an Ireland consolation but Liam Daish hits his shot wide from Gary Kelly's free kick.

63 Minutes – Quinn must score! But he doesn't, because Dion Dublin comes up with an unbelievable block. Phil Babb heads the resulting corner tamely at David Seaman.

66 Minutes – **SUBSTITUTION**
Double change for England, with Paul Scholes and Steve McManaman rested. Michael Owen and Darren Eadie are on in their place.

72 Minutes – **YELLOW CARD**. Liam Daish is fouled by Rio Ferdinand and the young Englishman is booked.

83 Minutes – **YELLOW CARD**. Gazza! When will you learn? Paul Gascoigne started this all off at Wembley but he is booked for dissent to end it.

FULL TIME – Ireland 0 – 3 England (England win 0-4 on Aggregate)

ENGLAND QUALIFY FOR THE 1998 WORLD CUP
It's all over – a quiet final twenty minutes but the damage was done early on, and then sealed with a brilliant David Beckham goal. All eyes will be on the draw now as England can start to plan next summer.

There's drama in the other playoff games, with Bulgaria knocking out Croatia on penalties. Croatia finished 3rd in the real World Cup with Davor Suker getting the Golden Boot, but that's all out the window now. Switzerland knock out future European Championship co-hosts Austria after an epic penalty shootout, 11-10 the final penalty score. It's a lot simpler for Belgium as they triumph 4-0 on aggregate against Ukraine.

It's time for the draw, England are second seeds which should help. Denmark, Chile and Romania will be our opponents, which could be a lot worse. Denmark and Romania are both more than decent though, as England found out in real life where Dan Petrescu broke English hearts and left us facing Argentina. There's yet another friendly in December, people complain about International Football in the modern game but it's nowhere near as prominent as it is here.

More midweek shenanigans and Man Utd are back to winning ways, triumphing 4-2 at the Dell. Arsenal draw 1-1 at 6th placed Blackburn to give Man Utd their 9th point lead back. There's eight points between Arsenal and North London rivals Spurs in 3rd, but there's only seven points between 3rd and 14th placed West Ham. Crystal Palace lose 2-0 at home to Newcastle to slip six points adrift of safety with only one win so far. In Spain, both Barcelona and Real Madrid advance to the Copa de Rey 4th round after wins over Betis and Zaragoza respectively.

Saturday is here again and it is nearly a second consecutive 0-0 draw at Old Trafford, but Teddy Sheringham scores a late goal to beat Leicester. Arsenal, Chelsea & Tottenham all win to maintain their positions. An improving Newcastle win 1-0 at Blackburn, despite Kenny Dalglish pairing Des Hamilton with Steve Watson up front. I don't know why. Alan Shearer is a month away from a return which is good news for me as England manager but also for people who don't like to see crimes against football such as Des Hamilton starting in the Premier League. It's a bad weekend for Real Madrid, losing 3-2 to Compostela drops them down to 4th as Barcelona, Betis & Valencia all climb above them.

We're at match day five in the Champions League and Newcastle are the first to book their place in the last eight, beating Tiligul Tiraspol of Moldova 4-0. Des Hamilton scores twice and gets man of the match. Rangers are in trouble as they lose 3-1 away in Dortmund, but Man Utd are all but through after a 3-0 win over CSKA Sofia. Paul Scholes scored twice taking his tally for the season to twenty-one in just twenty three games. Juventus and Real Madrid both win to leave Juventus one point ahead going into the final game in that group, it looks likely we will lose one of those two big hitters. It's a similar story for Barcelona and Bayern Munich, where Bayern lead by three points with one game to play. The last game though will see the German giants travel to the Nou Camp in a mouth watering shootout.

Leeds need something different to get them out of the bottom three and they've taken a punt on Duncan Ferguson. £4.2m is not a bad price for big Dunc, who turns down West Ham in the process. I'm sure Harry thought he was a terrific footballer as well. The world wants to see the Hasselbaink/Ferguson combination so we'll look out for that one.

The last weekend of November is here and Blackburn assume the position of the best of the rest after a 1-0 win at Villa. Tottenham's 0-0 draw at Wimbledon drops them to 4th, whilst Leeds hold Chelsea to a 1-1 draw at Elland Road on Ferguson's debut, though he played no part in the goal. They're still in the bottom three though, alongside Bolton and perennial losers Crystal Palace. A thrilling day in Scotland sees the Old firm each draw their games 0-0 whilst over in Spain, Real Madrid beat Real Betis to take back 2nd spot behind Barcelona, who win again.

That rounds off the month though, with Kenny Dalglish taking Manager of the Month due to their Champions League form and for allowing Des Hamilton to score a Champions League goal. George Graham takes it again in Scotland whilst van Gaal is the victor in Spain. However, it's time to get those decorations up...

December

The coveted World Club Cup is won by Sao Paulo on penalties against Borussia Dortmund. Germans losing on penalties? The game is broken. It is a series of Germans who miss the penalties as well – Lars Ricken, Jürgen Kohler and Jorg Heinrich the culprits. Sao Paulo only have four "real" players – for teams in unplayable leagues or even some unloaded leagues, not all the squad are in the game or loaded so the remaining places are made up of fictional "greyed out" players who can't be signed. In that respect, it's a really bad result for Dortmund.

It's time to name my squad for the upcoming friendly with Holland, I don't give friendlies the time of the day so a quick courtesy glance at my squad tells me nobody is injured and Shearer isn't yet ready to return, so no changes are made. I am spoilt for choice though up front, five of the top six scorers in the Premier League are English – Scholes, Wright, Fowler, Ferdinand and Sheringham. When you think of what England had then to what they have now, it's no wonder we consider that our national team is in decline.

At Hampden Park it's the Scottish Coca-Cola Cup final between Celtic and Rangers. As has been the way so far, Rangers run out comfortable 2-0 winners and Andy Goram lifts the trophy. In England, the same competition is at the last sixteen stage, and there's somewhat of a shock when Middlesbrough knock out Liverpool 2-1 at the Riverside, Gianluca Festa with the 90th minute winner. Boro have the quite ridiculous pairing of Branca and Shevchenko up front, depending on whether he is the real deal or not. Man Utd are on the verge of going out as they are taken to penalties by ten man Tottenham, Ramon Vega seeing red after just twenty two minutes. Dion Dublin misses the 5th penalty but then so does Ian Walker, allowing Sheringham to score and Nicola Berti to miss to get Man Utd out of jail. Division Three Torquay are thumped 4-0 at The Dell, but they'll be delighted to make it this far.

The weekend arrives with the news Gareth Southgate is out injured for a few weeks and will miss the Holland friendly. Whatever. Wimbledon roll back the clock to 1988 and beat Liverpool 2-0, this time at Anfield. Spurs beat Leeds 1-0 despite Ramon Vega collecting his second red card in three days, so much for the Swiss being neutral. The big news though comes at Old Trafford, where the Champions are finally beaten, and by their nearest rivals too. Arsenal go 2-0 up inside eight minutes and then get battered for the remaining eighty two, but only concede once to a Paul Scholes penalty and it's a big win that could either breathe life in the title race, or just make the Red Devils even angrier. Sheffield Wednesday have snuck up into fourth, courtesy of a late Niclas Alexandersson winner against Newcastle. Alexandersson is a massive favourite of fans of the game due to being able to play every outfield position, the only man to have this trait other than Luis Enrique of Barcelona. At the time of writing, he is their manager.

The UEFA Cup last eight is set, with Celtic defying their domestic form to knock Nantes out 3-0 on aggregate. In an all English clash, Liverpool edge through against Leicester despite a Steve Claridge double, whilst Arsenal knock out Auxerre impressively. Udinese cause an upset in the all Italian contest against Inter Milan, whose squad includes Ronaldo and a very young Javier Zanetti. Liverpool vs Ajax is the pick of the quarter finals.

That big Champions League shootout between Barcelona and Bayern Munich is here! Typically, it finishes 0-0 which eliminates Barcelona. Their Spanish rivals Real Madrid are also out,nine points seeing them finish second to Juventus. Monaco and Dortmund both make it out of Group B, Dortmund the holders sneaking through as one of the two best runners up. Parma have blown it though, losing to Sporting Lisbon sees them slip to 2nd and they haven't done enough to go through. PSG do sneak through despite finishing 2nd to Man Utd, whilst Newcastle are denied a 100% record with a 1-1 draw against PSV. The Quarter Final draw sees a repeat of the 1997 final with Juventus playing Dortmund, whilst Bayern Munich take on Man Utd. Newcastle vs Monaco and Sporting Lisbon vs. PSG round off the draw. All European competitions are now on hold until March.

Sunderland signs Lars Bohinen for £2.6m. Not only has Lars dropped down a division, he's turned down 4th placed Sheffield Wednesday in the process. Sunderland have built up a six point lead at the top of Division One, so it probably won't be long before the Norwegian International is a Premier League player again.

International friendlies are the order of the weekend and I have that trip to Holland. We pick up where we left off in Ireland and score three times in the opening ten minutes against a very strong Holland side – and Ed de Goey. Robbie Fowler scores once and Steve McManaman twice in an impressive win, capped off by Dion Dublin getting a perfect ten rating at centre back. I don't know why Dion is playing like Baresi in this particular save, he's always good but never this good!

This could be a game changer – Peter Schmeichel is ruled out for a year with a broken pelvis. From a selfish point of view, it should make Denmark weaker next summer but I wonder if Manchester United will go and buy a goalkeeper? It doesn't affect Manchester United straight away – Kevin Pilkington stepping in to keep a clean sheet at home to Everton. Leeds earn a priceless win at Anfield, but it's not enough to move them out of the bottom three. Arsenal can only draw 0-0 at Leicester though, so Man Utd still hold an eight point lead. It's Old Firm day again in Scotland, this time at Ibrox. Celtic claim a creditable 1-1 draw thanks to a Stephen Glass equaliser but they drop to 6th. Hibs are Rangers' closest challengers but are six points adrift. It's as you were in Spain with both Barcelona and Real Madrid winning.

Happy Christmas! Or more accurately, happy football day as the traditional Boxing day games arrive in England and Scotland. The Spanish take a few weeks off at this time of year, but I refuse to imagine a world with no Boxing Day games. The big game of the day sees Man Utd travel to rapidly improving Newcastle, who are 5th. It ends in a hard fought 1-1 draw. Arsenal fail to take advantage though, only drawing 1-1 at home to bottom club Palace. Liverpool are down to 10th after losing 1-0 away at Chelsea. Celtic climb up to 5th in Scotland after Henrik Larsson's late penalty helps them beat Motherwell.

There's one more game though before the end of 1997. Newcastle and Manchester United have had a game in hand since Newcastle played a Champions League qualifier instead of their league fixture all the way back in August. It means they rather strangely play each other twice in the space of five days, but Newcastle pull off the win thanks to Gary Speed (RIP). The manager of the month awards are handed out, and the three league leaders take the prizes – Ferguson, Smith & van Gaal.

January

The first weekend in January is the traditional home of FA Cup 3rd round day and this game is no different, with the usual array of David vs Goliath encounters as well as some other intriguing matches. Division 3 Colchester hold Aston Villa to a 1-1 draw, Gareth Southgate salvaging a replay twenty minutes from time. There's an eye catching result at Stamford Bridge. Keegan's stamp is all over this match as Chelsea beat Scunthorpe 6-3, Mark Hughes helping himself to a hat trick. Leicester are upset at home after losing 1-0 to First division Stockport, and Wimbledon beat Crystal Palace 3-1 in the Selhurst derby. Alan Shearer is back in action for Newcastle and scores twice in a 4-1 win at WBA. In Scotland, it's a regular day of league fixtures, with Rangers once again winning and remaining unbeaten. The game of the day comes at Tannadice, where Celtic come from 3-1 down to win 4-3 and lift themselves up to 4th. George Graham – Entertainer.

There's a real cup theme about the place at the minute, as the midweek fixtures not only see the League Cup Quarter finals but also the European Super Cup first leg between Barcelona and Borussia Dortmund. This game is played out between the Champions League Winners and the Cup Winners Cup winners, and is of course now no longer played due to the cancellation of the Cup Winners Cup in favour of the behemoth that is the Europa League. There is of course a Super Cup played in August each year between the Champions League &

Europa League winners, but it is only over one leg in a neutral venue. Anyway, after all of that, Barcelona win 1-0 thanks to Ivan de la Pena's goal.

The League Cup Quarter Finals looked quite dull on paper but Arsenal find Keith Branagan in inspired from and then lose to a Nathan Blake goal in extra time to be knocked out in front of their own fans by Bolton. Manchester United win 2-0 at Leicester, whilst Manchester neighbours City beat Southampton 2-1 at Maine Road to set up a two legged semi-final with Blackburn, who knocked out Middlesbrough.

Raimond van der Gouw is not as good as Peter Schmeichel. Ian Taylor is the beneficiary, as Villa steal a 2-2 draw at Old Trafford. Arsenal capitalise, but only just, as Ian Wright scores a 90th minute winner against a dogged West Ham. The gap at the top is down to six points, whilst Tottenham in 3rd are under increasing pressure from Sheffield Wednesday. Duncan Ferguson scores his first goal for Leeds, a vital winner in a 3-2 victory at Blackburn. It's still not enough to lift Leeds out of the bottom three, though they are now at least level with Leicester. In Scotland, Rangers lose their first game of the season at home to Aberdeen, but they still hold a nine point advantage over Hibs. It's a good win for Barcelona in Spain, winning 3-1 away to Valencia but Real Madrid keep the gap at three points after easily beating Mallorca at the Bernabeu.

Paul Ince's hip has given out and he'll be side lined for four months. That makes him a massive doubt for the World Cup and he was already a maybe anyway. To be honest, we've absolutely murdered *Three Lions 98* – it's going to have to be entirely re-written. For starters, that night in Rome was very poor but we did have a jolly fine time in Ireland. If you're confused what I'm talking about, the famous *Three Lions* song (Football's Coming Home) that was released for Euro 96 had a spruce up for World Cup 1998 and became a hit all over again. More on that later though.

The glimmer of hope Arsenal had earned themselves has evaporated – the gap is back to eight points after the Gunners can only draw 1-1 at Everton whilst Man Utd ease to victory at Derby. Shearer nets another two goals, this time against Crystal Palace, to move Newcastle into the "best of the rest" position of 3rd. North East rivals Sunderland move six points clear, Pierre van Hooijdonk has proven to be a shrewd signing by Peter Reid.

Rangers win at Hibs, to move nine points clear of Aberdeen, though the battle for 2nd is far more interesting with just three points between the Dons and Hibs in 5th. Celtic are 3rd. Barcelona can only draw 0-0 at Deportivo, who are 3rd, but Real Madrid are in Copa del Rey action so the gap is temporarily four points. I've neglected the Copa del Rey so far, and with FA Cup 4th round weekend imminent, now is a good time to get you caught up. The Spanish Cup sees every round played over two legs but they don't have a league cup equivalent, they just play twice as many games in the other cup. The semi finals have actually thrown up two derbies – Barcelona vs Espanyol and Real Madrid vs Atletico Madrid. They aren't played until April though, meaning there's three months between the Quarter finals and the semis. At least that will give the police plenty time to prepare.

I would love it if we beat them! Keegan sleighs the demons of 1996 as his Chelsea side knock Manchester United out of the FA Cup in the 4th round. To rub salt into Peter Schmeichel's pelvic wound, former Red Mark Hughes scores an 88th minute winner to secure a 3-2 win and send Stamford Bridge tepid. Arsenal had the much easier task of disposing of Lincoln at Highbury, and thanks to a Dennis Bergkamp hat-trick, they manage. No such thing as squad rotation for the cup back in these days, the way it should be. Division One Tranmere knock out Leeds at Prenton Park, young Northern Irishman Darren Fitzgerald (on loan from Rangers) scores the winner in injury time. Regular players of the game will know the value of having Fitzgerald on loan in the lower leagues, the boy doesn't miss. No games in Scotland but Barcelona & Real Madrid win, so very little to report elsewhere.

The reason there were no games in Scotland is that it's their FA Cup 3rd round day on Sunday. I'm not sure why they wait to the Sunday. Rangers are knocked out by Motherwell and champagne corks are popped by the other Scottish Premier clubs who might actually have a chance now. One of those clubs though won't be Celtic, who are knocked out 1-0 away at Division Two Livingston. It's perhaps telling that it wasn't deemed worthy of the "shock result" graphic. Hibs are out too, beaten at Falkirk, whilst Kilmarnock are thrashed 3-0 at home by Division One Raith Rovers. Aberdeen must be delighted.

Barcelona win the Super Cup, drawing the second leg 0-0 away in Germany. What an awful way to win it, 1-0 on aggregate over two legs. Two evenly matched sides or a lack of attacking tactics? Louis van Gaal manages Barcelona, so you decide.

Celtic move to resolve their crisis by signing Czech defender Jiri Novotny. It's a great deal at £1.1m but as a neutral observer, they've conceded as few as Rangers but scored plenty less, but I suppose it's asking a lot of George Graham to buy attackers.
Speaking of attackers, Blackburn sign Steve Slade from QPR. Slade had a one in two record in Division One for QPR so it makes sense, but isn't it a month late for Slade? Terrible jokes aside, they've paid £4.8m for him to partner Kevin Gallacher, as real life top scorer Chris Sutton plays at centre back with Colin Hendry. Roy Hodgson is still their manager, by the way.

Man Utd have had a full squad, which has inhibited them spending their £40m in the bank. Finally though they've shifted Brian McClair to Partick Thistle which allows them to sign Henk Fraser for £2.4m, turning down Atletico Madrid & Juventus to make the move to England. Fraser is a Dutch International centre back who can play left back, but he'll turn thirty two before the season is out so it's an odd signing. I assume they would buy to cover the stricken Schmeichel, but in Kevin Pilkington we trust apparently.

Hold on though, they've also flogged Denis Irwin! To Real Mallorca of all places. Irwin always took a decent penalty, which was odd given the amount of attacking talent they had. Anyway, presumably Fraser is in to replace him and we wait to see if Fergie moves for a keeper.

The end of January is a transfer deadline day across Europe, but not England, and there's a few players on the move. Juventus pay £7.5m for Giuseppe Signori, who is clinging on to being an Italian international but his best days are behind him. The big transfer of the day though is in Spain, where the original (and best) Ronaldo is on the move. £11.5m is a great price, and Real Madrid win out in the race with Barcelona, who had tried to bring back their former star. That is a massive game changer in the La Liga title race. Atletico Madrid don't like to be left out so they spend £9.5m on Portugal International Rui Costa from Fiorentina.

Manchester United are seemingly building a wall around Kevin Pilkington, paying £8.25m plus David May for Sol Campbell. Campbell is a key part of my England team, so I just hope they play him. What do Spurs want with David May? I mean, he *might* be the perfect partner for Ramon Vega, but I doubt it.

There's time for one more set of fixtures in January, with Arsenal cementing second spot with a 1-0 win over Newcastle at Highbury. Ian Wright with his twenty third goal of the season. Manchester United win by the same score line against Barnsley – they got seven in the same fixture in reality so Barnsley should be happy with themselves. Leeds are out of the bottom three after a 2-2 draw at Sheffield Wednesday. This drops Leicester into the mire after a 4-1 home reverse against Derby County. Leicester consider Pegguy Arphexad a star player but play Kasey Keller over him, so work that one out.

Arsene Wenger takes manager of the month, whilst Tommy McLean of Aberdeen takes it in Scotland and it's King Louis again in Spain.

February
Hold on to your hats, the qualifying groups for Euro 2000 are about to be drawn. In the unlikely event that there is demand for a sequel of this book, this would probably feature prominently. As it is, I'll just leave you with the news England will take on Northern Ireland, Bielorussia (Belarus if you're in the modern world), Lithuania and Romania. And this was never spoken of again.

Rangers sign French goalkeeper Mickael Landreau from Nantes for £3.7m. This might not seem like a big deal but I ran a feature on the blog where readers could nominate and vote for their favourite goalkeeper in the game and this chap won, so Rangers have got a real star – though he's only eighteen at the moment, so they'll have to commit to playing him. Andy Goram is older than time though, so it won't be long before he calls it a day.

Blackburn have obviously decided the football league is a treasure trove of talent, adding Tony Thorpe from

Fulham to their collection for £4.2m. I'm reliably informed Thorpe was nicknamed "The Luton Laudrup" when plying his trade at Kenilworth Road, so maybe Roy is wise after all.

The weekend's Premier League programme is hindered by the League Cup semi-finals taking place on Sunday, so there are only seven games. With Man Utd not playing, Arsenal have a free hit at cutting the gap but can only draw 0-0 at Aston Villa. Shearer scores twice again to take his tally to nine goals in ten games since his return, his side beating Everton 3-1. His form is great news for me as England boss but just about every England striker is in form. The bottom three is unchanged, with both Leeds & Leicester drawing their games 0-0. In Scotland, it's a good weekend for Celtic who beat Aberdeen 3-0 at Celtic Park. Aberdeen score two own goals in the first half and there's no coming back from that. Rangers can only draw 0-0 at Dundee Utd. Barcelona are off the top in Spain, Real Madrid winning their game in hand during the week and then today thrashing Celta Vigo. Barcelona drew 0-0 at home to Real's neighbours Atletico to surrender pole position.

The League Cup semi-final first legs go to form – Blackburn edging Division One Manchester City 1-0 thanks to Damien Duff, whilst Manchester United win 2-0 at Bolton, two of my England team Gary Neville and Paul Scholes on target.

Kevin Keegan isn't feeling the love on Valentine's day, his side are thrashed 4-1 at Stamford Bridge by former side Newcastle in the FA Cup 5th round. Division Two Fulham hold Arsenal 0-0 at Craven Cottage to earn a Highbury replay, which probably won't cause Arsene Wenger too much trouble. Division One Man City knock out Premier League Barnsley, though to be fair the Yorkshire club have barely won after their early season form tailed off. They sit 16th and haven't won in 11 league games. There is one Premier League game, but 18th placed Leicester miss the chance to break free of the bottom three by losing 2-0 at home to Wimbledon. Kinnear's men are up to 6th, maybe he did win all those awards after all? Celtic reclaim their second spot after a 1-0 win away at Hibs, the only league game in Scotland today. It's as you were in Spain as the big two both score easy away wins, with Ronaldo making his Real Madrid debut.

Liverpool advance to the FA Cup quarter final after being Blackburn 3-0, the game is played on the Sunday as Everton played at home on the Saturday. I'm a big fan of the small detail being in the game, so well played Sports Interactive. It's also cup day in Scotland, with Aberdeen winning at Hearts to cement their position as favourites. Dundee Utd will also be thereabouts, proven by their 3-0 win away at Premier League Dunfermline. Hearts actually won the trophy in the real world, so that's another thing that isn't happening.

It's another win for the small detail in midweek, as Manchester United vs Bolton in the League Cup semi-final second leg is brought forward a day to the Tuesday to avoid clashing with Man City's second leg tie. It almost works for Bolton, who take the lead through Jamie Pollock – you most likely remember Jamie Pollock for scoring an unbelievably skilful own goal. Think Gazza against Scotland but at the wrong end. Anyway, he scored at the right end here and reduced Bolton's deficit to 2-1 on aggregate, but that pesky Paul Scholes netted his 30th goal of the season to seal a 3-1 aggregate win for Man Utd and a Wembley date – but with who?

Blackburn Rovers. Roy Hodgson might be a little bit more used to managing at Wembley nowadays but I imagine it will be quite the thrill for him back in 1998 to lead his side out in the League Cup Final. They draw 1-1 at Maine Road, to go through 2-1 on aggregate. Gary Flitcroft the hero, though a young Michael Brown equalises for Man City on the night. For a Division One side, City can be very pleased with their cup run.

Who remembers who scored Scotland's goal in the opening game of the 1998 World Cup against Brazil? To those of you saying John Collins - congratulations. He's just signed for Manchester United from Monaco for £725,000. It's a cheap fee as his contract was running out, but I've always wondered how he ended up at Monaco in the first place. The Monaco team of this era is something else, with a forward line including Thierry Henry and David Trezeguet and a young Fabien Barthez in goal. Jean Tigana was the manager, who went on to manage Fulham a few years later. Come to think of it, he signed Collins for them too…

Sheffield Wednesday break out the 'Shock Defeat' graphic after a 3-0 triumph at Anfield. It lifts The Owls up to 6th and leaves Liverpool in 10th, which is disgraceful really when you consider the squad Roy Evans has. Arsenal close the gap to just five points after a 3 -0 win at Oakwell, whilst Man Utd only draw 0-0 at Chelsea. In the proverbial sixpointer at Elland Road, Andy Gray scores a priceless winner as Leeds beat Leicester 1-0. It's not the Andy Gray who was all over *Sky Sports* in this era, but a young Scot who'd go on to have a journeyman career. Palace lose the Selhurst derby 3-1, leaving them twelve points from safety. George Graham is the toast of Celtic as he leads his team to an Old Firm derby win – Henrik Larsson scores twice in a 3-1 victory. Rangers are still nine points ahead though, so it would be a big ask for Celtic to repeat their real life success. Barcelona are back on top of La Liga after Real Madrid can only draw with Valencia.

That's one defeat too many for Steve Coppell, a midweek defeat at home to Barnsley costs him his job. With three wins from twenty seven games and a massive fifty goals conceded, it's a wonder he wasn't sacked sooner. Elsewhere, Man Utd win away at in form Wimbledon to increase their lead back to eight points. Liverpool lose at home to Blackburn, in a game where Neil Ruddock was sent off after seven minutes. That lifts Rovers into the top six at Wimbledon's expense. Whilst these leagues games were being played, Arsenal were busy winning their cup replay with Fulham by a comfortable 2-0 score-line.

The last day of February sees the shock defeat headline rolled out again, this time at Highbury as Kinnear's

Wimbledon win thanks to a Michael Hughes goal. Manchester United miss the chance to extend their lead after being held 2-2 at Old Trafford by Tottenham. Roy Keane gets sent off, which is much less likely to shock anybody. Manager-less Crystal Palace lose 3-2 at home to Leeds, which leaves the Eagles fifteen points from safety. Leeds on the other hand are clawing themselves to safety at the expense of Martin O'Neill's Leicester, who lose 2-1 at home to Chelsea. Aberdeen continue to be the meat in the Old Firm sandwich in Scotland, whilst Barcelona & Real Madrid both win over in Spain.

The England board are satisfied with my performance, then again I haven't done anything for three months. Future England manager Roy Hodgson takes manager of the month in the Premier League, whilst it's a repeat of January in Scotland and Spain as McLean & Van Gaal take the awards again.

March
Crystal Palace about Roy Aitken to replace Steve Coppell. Aitken is a young manager who only finished playing in 1995 before becoming Aberdeen manager, where he left in 1997. It's a very left field appointment to say the least, but it's nice to see some different names cropping up.

Well look what came crawling back! European competition kicks off again with the UEFA Cup quarter final first legs, and Arsenal have bounced back from their Wimbledon humbling with an impressive 2-1 win at Kaiserslautern. Ian Wright's twenty sixth of the season helps the Gunners on their way. It's less good for Liverpool who are held 1-1 at Anfield by Ajax, whilst Celtic draw 2-2 at home to Metz. Hassan Kachloul scores twice for Metz, who fans of Southampton will remember for being moderately successful there. The final tie sees Udinese beaten 2-1 at home by Bordeaux.

As is tradition, the Champions League is scheduled the following day and although both Spanish giants are out, England still have two representatives. Manchester United, without the injured Paul Scholes for the next month, lose 1-0 away to Bayern Munich but they'll not be too upset with only a one goal deficit. Newcastle's first leg sees them welcome Monaco to St James' Park and the game finishes 2-2, Andreas Andersson scoring twice for the Magpies but two young Frenchmen by the names of Henry & Giuly are on the scoresheet for Monaco. The repeat of last year's final between Dortmund and Juventus finishes 0-0, but that always looked like a close game. The most one sided tie of the round sees PSG take a 3-0 lead over Sporting Lisbon – they'll be confident of getting the job finished in Portugal.

If the UEFA Cup is the proverbial starter course, then the Cup Winners Cup is definitely the dessert. Very tempting but are you too full? It's no wonder it was eventually done away with.

Chelsea get a creditable 1-1 draw away to Real Betis – the Blues won the trophy this season in reality, so they're well on the way to repeating that. They played out a classic semi-final with Vicenza of Italy, who hold a 1-0 lead over Stuttgart who were actually the beaten finalists. Elsewhere Sparta Prague thrash the brilliantly named Germinal Ekeren 4-1, whilst Fenerbahce and AEK Athens draw 2-2 in Turkey.

The big problem with Thursday night football is the impact on the weekend games. Back in 1998, the game either hasn't taken it into account or fatigue meant nothing to these people as forty eight hours after the Betis draw, Chelsea are back at Stamford Bridge ruining Roy Aitken's debut with a 1-0 win. It's a limited Premier League programme as it's also FA Cup Quarter Final day. John Aldridge is a thirty nine year old player-manager of Division One Tranmere, but he classes himself as a star player and he underlines that status by scoring the winner against Sheffield Wednesday. Ian Wright nets yet again as Arsenal see off Everton, but Liverpool and Newcastle can only draw 0-0 at Anfield. The real excitement is at Maine Road, where Premier League West Ham blow a 2-0 lead allowing First Division Man City claim a 3-2 win. Former England man Nigel Clough is amongst the scorers for Joe Royle's men. It's cup weekend in Scotland so the only game is a 1-1 draw at Rugby Park between Kilmarnock and Rangers, and you'll never guess what happens in La Liga – the big two win again!

Remember when I said Aberdeen were favourites for the Scottish Cup? I'd like to revise that as they are humbled 4-0 away at Dundee Utd. The Tangerines are the only Premier League side in the semi finals, as Division Two Clydebank stun Motherwell 2-1 at Fir Park. Division One club Airdrie – the original, before it was liquidated in 2002 – win 3-1 at Premier League St

Johnstone to continue the madness. Hamilton (Division One) and Livingston (Division Two) play out a 0-0 draw and will replay.

There's a midweek bonus as the top two in the Premier League have catch up games. Manchester United struggle without Scholes, pairing Dublin & Sheringham up top but drawing 0-0 with an improving Leeds. That allows Arsenal to cut the lead to seven points after they batter Derby 1-0. Mart Poom saves eight shots but Patrick Vieira finds the way through eventually. Bolton remain 19th after losing 1-0 at home to Liverpool, though they do still have another game in hand.

We're back to a full complement of weekend fixtures, and the highlight in the Premier League is 2nd vs 4th as Arsenal welcome Chelsea. A Dennis Bergkamp double helps the Gunners win 2-1, but it doesn't gain them any ground as Manchester United thump Coventry 4-0. The bottom three all lose, Crystal Palace seem to have been on fourteen points forever, eight adrift of Bolton and Leicester who aren't exactly motoring away themselves. Rangers win away at Aberdeen, and with Celtic thrashing Hearts, the Old Firm are reunited as the top two. Barcelona and Real Madrid both edge 1-0 wins, just a point separate the two giants but they have a thirteen point cushion back to 3rd placed Betis.

I'm invited to pick my England squad for the friendly with Norway. Scholes will just about make it back and I'll have Shearer for the first time, but after the impressive performances in the second leg against Ireland and the friendly with Holland, I probably won't change too much. I'm tempted to have a look at Ian

Wright, who with twenty seven goals has only three less than Scholes. Heskey has only netted six in Scotland, so he's out.

UEFA Cup day again and it's a terrible day for British Clubs, with all three bowing out. Ajax need extra time to knock out Liverpool, but future Rangers player Shota Arveladze scores the winner. Arsenal lose 2-0 at home to Kaiserslautern to exit the competition 3-2 on aggregate, whilst Kachloul scores again as Metz triumph 4-2 on aggregate against Celtic. Bordeaux knock out Udinese after a 0-0 draw in France.

Newcastle continue the theme for English clubs, going out on away goals in Monaco. A bizarre games finishes 0-0 where the home side have 0 shots on goal. Newcastle themselves only manage two in what must have been a riveting encounter. Man Utd keep the flag flying though, knocking out Bayern Munich with a 2-0 win on the night – Dion Dublin with the winner. Remember, the Red Devils have Kevin Pilkington in goal, so this is frankly a miracle. Juventus bring Dortmund's reign to a sorry end by thrashing them 3-0 to gain revenge for the final defeat, whilst PSG ease through 4-1 on aggregate over Sporting Lisbon. In some bonus Premier League games, Spurs regain 4th after a 2-0 win over beleaguered Bolton, whilst Livingston win that mouth-watering Quarter final replay against Hamilton.

A glum week for English football is rounded off by Chelsea, thrashed 4-1 at home by Betis to go out of the Cup Winners Cup. Stuttgart keep up their end of the bargain though and see of Vicenza, and Fenerbahce get a good win in Athens. Sparta Prague complete the semi-final line up after a 6-3 thrashing of Germinal Ekeren, who have done Belgium proud. The bad week for English football is rounded off with the news that Gazza has strained his back and will miss the Norway game.

Rather strangely, there are no games in the top division this weekend. There are International friendlies scheduled midweek, is that a reason to have no games? I can't offer an explanation. Newcastle tried to break the monotony by bidding £3.1m for Liverpool's underused midfielder Jamie Redknapp, whilst not to be outdone, North East neighbours Sunderland purchase Marcus Stewart from Huddersfield. This actually did happen in real life a few years later.

Unsurprisingly, it's all a big waste of time in Norway and we play out a tepid 0-0 draw. The positive is we restricted Norway to a single shot, whilst we managed 6 but only hit the target once. Sheringham and Wright started up front but neither shone, whilst we missed Gazza in the middle of the park. Ronny Johnsen got man of the match. Let's go home. We go to Spain in a month for another kick about.

Blackburn aren't satisfied with Steve Slade so move for Andy Cole. That happened in real life too, but Cole had scored a lot more goals for Man Utd by the time he left Old Trafford. QPR and Sheff Wed were also in for Cole but he opts for Blackburn in a £3.4m move. Cole's career has always been confusing to me – he scored so many goals at club level but got so little International recognition. I suppose as you've seen already, the calibre of strikers in England was so high during this era.

We've arrived at Friday 27th March 1998 – why is that important? Well, other than being my Mam's birthday, it's transfer deadline day in Britain. Long before *Sky Sports News* and Twitter, the last Friday in March was that final chance to get somebody through the door to help you achieve your goals. To be honest, it was mostly loan deals for football league clubs but there is the odd transfer rushed through. Here, Manchester United continue to build an impenetrable wall around Kevin Pilkington by adding Lillian Thuram to their defence. £5m is a great price for a defender who went on to have a great World Cup in his home country and of course ended up winning the tournament, whether he replicates that success where it really matters (this game) remains to be seen. The Red Devils also sign Patrick Andersson from Borussia Monchengladbach for £3.2m – yet another centre back, this time a Swedish International, it's really gone beyond a joke. The centre halves available are now: Johnsen, Fraser, Dublin, G Neville, Berg, Campbell, Andersson, Thuram, Pallister and a very young Wes Brown. Pilkington between the sticks though.

Newcastle are busy too, pulling off the surprise capture of Leonardo from AC Milan for £3.4m. For a full Brazil International, it's a ridiculous signing. They follow that up with the signing of Jamie Redknapp from Liverpool for £3.1m. Redknapp has barely featured for Liverpool – and he hasn't even been injured. If he performs well, he has a shot of making my World Cup squad because he could be useful back up to Gascoigne. A Geordie is on the move as Michael Bridges makes the move to Rangers from Sunderland. Moving for £3.3m, Bridges becomes the latest to turn down Sheffield Wednesday. That wraps up deadline day though, with more action than I anticipated!

Stop everything – Crystal Palace have won! Andy Linighan scores to secure a famous 1-0 win at Anfield of all places. Liverpool remain 10th and well below expectation. Man Utd don't have the chance to show off their wall of defenders ad they have the League Cup final tomorrow, so Arsenal take the opportunity to cut the gap with a 2-1 win away at local rivals Tottenham. Newcastle go back to playing Steve Watson up front with Shearer and both score in a 2-1 win at Leeds to keep the Magpies 3rd. Bolton hammer Southampton 5-1, thirty-seven-year-old Peter Beardsley rolling back the years, to bring them within six points of Barnsley, who have fallen to 17th after a dreadful run. North of the border and all of Celtic's recent hard work is undone with a 2-1 loss at St Johnstone. Rangers thrash Hibs 4-1 and the title will almost certainly be heading to Ibrox. The Madrid derby ends in a draw at the Bernabeu as Vieri cancels out Ronaldo's opener. That allows Barcelona to extend their lead, Sonny Anderson is keeping Alfonso out of the team with his current form, highlighted by his 12th and 13th goals of the season here in only his 17th game.

The first domestic trophy of the season (sorry Charity Shield fans) is up for grabs as Blackburn take on Man Utd at Wembley. Blackburn actually dominate the game but can find no way past Kevin Pilkington, who after all the stick I have given him ends up saving two penalties in the shootout and taking man of the match. One of those penalties was from Andy Cole, who has been a Blackburn player for all of four days. Scholes, Beckham & Sheringham all score their penalties in the shootout, which bodes well for the National team. 0-0 in a cup final is never nice to see but the drama of penalties makes up for it. The final in real life was also a 0-0 between Chelsea and Division One Middlesbrough, but two extra time goals settled it in Chelsea's favour.

The UEFA Cup semi-final first legs round off the month, Bordeaux beating Kaiserslautern 1-0 and Metz springing a bit of a surprise by beating Ajax 3-0. The second legs will follow in a few weeks.
The manager gongs are given to Ferguson, McGhee (Dundee Utd) and Aragones (Real Betis) for their varying cup successes during the month. Advancing in the latter stages of the cups is worth more 'performance points' and the most performance points in the month wins the award, so it becomes quite predictable who will win at this time of year.

April
Dion Dublin scores the winner in Monaco – not an April Fool's gag, it actually happened. A priceless 1-0 win for Man Utd in the Principality sets them up nicely for the second leg and potentially a place in the final. PSG hold Juventus to a 0-0 draw in Turin, which makes the French side slight favourites in the return legs. There's also an FA Cup replay – Newcastle scrape past Liverpool at St James' Park thanks to Alan Shearer.

Dalglish opts for thirty six year old Ian Rush to partner Shearer presumably as part of some sort of lost bet, but it's irrelevant as the Magpies advance to a semi-final with Tranmere. The semi-finals are played at neutral venues – not Wembley – which in my opinion are the way it should be. Getting to Wembley would be a lot bigger deal if you didn't play the semi-finals there too.

Anyway, in about four days, Newcastle will take on Tranmere at Old Trafford and Arsenal will play Man City at Anfield in the semis.

The Copa del Rey is back! Several months after the quarter finals, the hotly anticipated semi-finals are here. In the Catalan derby, Sonny Anderson underlines his new found form with a hat trick as Barcelona triumph 3-1 over Espanyol. Espanyol will get a chance for revenge in the return leg but they'll have their work cut out. The Madrid derby is a much duller affair, with Real sneaking a 1-0 advantage on home soil. Incidentally, Ronaldo has only played three times since his big move. The rule in Spain is you are allowed four non-EU players in your match day squad – Real Madrid have eight on the books, and Ronaldo seems to be behind Suker, Mijatovic, Roberto Carlos and Cesar Prates in the running. Ronaldo was widely regarded as the best striker in the world at this time, so this is quite a surprise.

There's a disrupted Premier League programme as there will be FA Cup semi-finals the following day, but Manchester United take the opportunity to extend their lead with a 1-0 win at Bolton. With Arsenal and

Newcastle otherwise engaged, Tottenham take the opportunity to leapfrog the Magpies into 3rd with a crushing 3-0 win at Everton. Barnsley pull themselves away from danger by defeating West Ham 2-1, which drops Leeds back down to 17th. They have 5 points over Bolton and with just 6 games to go, they should be ok. Celtic score 5 in their win at Dunfermline but Rangers also win, with Heskey on the scoresheet. The big two have the day off in Spain after their cup efforts the previous night.

Is there anything more annoying than an FA Cup semi-final replay? Fortunately it doesn't happen nowadays, but that is what Arsenal & Man City face in three days' time. City were actually seconds away from a famous win – Uwe Rosler's 83rd minute penalty gave them a lead, only to concede a stoppage time penalty that Ian Wright scored to keep Arsenal's hopes of replicating their real life cup success alive. Wright seems to score a stoppage time goal most weeks, it seems. At Old Trafford, Newcastle secure a nervy 1-0 win over Tranmere, thanks to Alan Shearer. We could yet have a repeat of the 1998 final where Arsenal defeated Newcastle 2-0.

The Scottish FA Cup semi-finals take place on the Monday – it's a week too early to be Easter so goodness knows why. Anyway, the season is so far on in Scotland, Livingston have already earned promotion from Division Two, meaning their 2-2 draw with Clydebank is a bit of a surprise. Clydebank are going to finish 3rd in the same division but are seventeen points adrift. Anyway, they'll replay. In the marginally less offensive semi-final, the only remaining Premier League side Dundee Utd are held 0-0 by Airdrie, who have actually already won Division One and will be playing in the Premier League next season. Two replays to look forward to.

Late drama at Anfield! It doesn't involve Liverpool though, but Man City cause a bit of a shock by knocking Arsenal out through a late Nigel Clough goal. Seaman sees red and Rosler converts the penalty, but Ian Wright's 31st goal of the season looked set to take it to extra time. Clough Junior pops up late on to send the blue half of Manchester potty. The other side of Manchester are pretty happy too – in the end. In their league game at Blackburn, former Red Andy Cole puts his new side 2-0 up but Giggs and Sheringham seal a point and a five point gap with seven to play. Barnsley beat Leeds 2-1 to keep the pressure on Victor Fernandez. Those highly anticipated Scottish Cup replays are both very one sided, Dundee Utd triumphing 4-1 whilst Livingston win 4-0. It's not a glamorous final but try telling that to those two teams!

Newcastle don't take kindly to being knocked out of 3rd, so retaliate by winning 1-0 at Tottenham to reclaim it. The evergreen John Barnes with the goal. Man Utd continue their winning ways with a 2-0 win at Sheffield Wednesday, and incredibly Arsenal win 1-0 via a last minute Ian Wright goal! It's almost predictable. Bolton vs Leicester is the proverbial two bald men fighting over a comb as they sit 18th and 19th in the table, so perhaps a 0-0 draw is a fitting result. Leeds secure a priceless 1-0 win over Derby to ease their worries and increase West Ham's very slightly, who now sit 17th albeit with a seven point gap. Celtic, Rangers, Real Madrid & Barcelona all win to maintain the status quo in our other leagues.

Oldham win the Windscreen shield! Andy Ritchie gets the winner in the final, sending Bristol City to defeat. This tournament has had numerous sponsors down the years but it's currently (2015) *Johnstone's Paint*, I'll let you decide if that is a step up from *Auto Windscreens.*

Easter Monday means more football – two games in three days no less. It turns out to be a significant day, as Arsenal are beaten 1-0 at home by Blackburn Rovers. David Seaman is sent off again – should he really be my number one for the World Cup? Manchester United pile on the misery with a 3-2 win over Southampton. Manchester United have defended well for months but apparently can't handle Carlton Palmer. Spurs are back up to 3rd as Newcastle are surprisingly beaten 1-0 at home by Liverpool, who sit 9th. Bolton win at Palace to cut their deficit to 4 points, but that loss relegates Crystal Palace. Sunderland will replace them, after thrashing QPR 3-0 and clocking up eighty six points. With 4 games to go, they could get close to the ton. Celtic can only draw at Aberdeen, whilst Rangers win to open up a twelve point gap. With only twelve points available, it's all over bar the shouting.

With the World Cup in France on the way, it seems quite fitting that we have an all French UEFA Cup final. Metz get a 2-2 draw in Amsterdam, allowing them to get through 5-2. The damage was done in the first leg, and Ajax never looked likely to overturn it. French legend Jean-Pierre Papin, now thirty four, scores the winner on the night as Bordeaux win 2-1 away at Kaiserslautern to set up the final in Frankfurt in early May.

It's time to pick my England squad for the friendly in Spain. Back in 1998, Spain had yet to really make their mark on a major tournament despite having a team full of stars. In terms of my squad, Ian Walker is out injured so Nigel Martyn is in. There's a doubt over Beckham but he might recover so I'll leave him in.

Before those pesky Internationals though, there's a Champions League Final to arrange. Juventus snatch a 1-1 draw in Paris to scrape through on away goals. The real life runners-up will have different opponents though, with Manchester United beating Monaco 2-0 with goals from Scholes and young Grant Brebner. It seems Brebner never made an appearance for Man Utd in real life but played well over a hundred times for Hibs. This is actually his debut and he's helped his side to a Champions League final, the stuff of dreams. It does mean though that Kevin Pilkington is on the verge of winning the Champions League. Only one game in the Premier League, Arsenal close the gap back to five points with a win over Liverpool. Man Utd have a game in hand to extend that lead once more though.

Tony Adams damaged his neck in that win and will be out for month. I could replace him but I'll most likely give Rio or Keown a chance to shine, so I'm not worried.

The Cup Winners Cup brings a night of drama, firstly Sparta Prague need penalties to see off Stuttgart and deny them a repeat of their final appearance. Real Betis draw 0-0 with Fenerbahce to sneak through on away goals and secure their place in the Stadio Olimpico next month.

Whilst Betis fly the flag for Spain in Europe, the battle is on to win the Copa de Rey. Espanyol beat Barcelona 1-0 but go out 3-2 on aggregate, but we are denied an El Clasico final as Kiko and Vieri score a goal each to help Atletico topple their illustrious neighbours.

Rangers win the Scottish Premier League! A 2-1 win at Hearts secures the title despite Celtic's win. It means Rangers get their 10th title in a row, something Wim Jansen's Celtic managed to arrest in real life, but Jansen barely lasted two months this time around. Back in England, Arsenal cling on to Man Utd's coat tails with a 1-0 win over Bolton. Wright decides to score about seventy minutes sooner than normal this time. With Bolton losing it gives West Ham the chance to all but secure safety, and although they twice lead at home to Man Utd, Paul Scholes' 32nd and 33rd goals of the season help his side to a 3-2 win.

It's a very quiet midweek as players head off for the International Friendlies this weekend, the only news of note is Darren Eadie picking up a two week injury which renders him unavailable for the Spain game. That wouldn't have been a problem but I'm bizarrely not allowed to pick Paul Merson on the day of the game as he has a club match. Middlesbrough being in Division One has scuppered that particular plan. I'm giving Flowers a go in goal and restoring the Scholes/Fowler front two which has performed pretty well.

That was an eye opener. England actually had the better of it for the most of the first seventy minutes but that greatly versatile man Luis Enrique scored twice as Alfonso added a third late on. Our big problem was finishing – ten shots and only one on target, oh dear. It's the last friendly before I name the squad and I'm not confident of even getting out of the group, let alone avenging our heroic penalty defeat.

Is this a lifeline for Arsenal? Man Utd can only draw at home to Crystal Palace, John Collins sparing their blushes after the already relegated side take the lead through Attilio Lombardo. Arsenal blow their big chance though, only drawing 1-1 at the Dell. Looking at the stats, they were even lucky to draw. Newcastle tighten their grip on 3rd with a 2-0 win over Chelsea, in what was no doubt an emotional night for Kevin Keegan. Manchester City secure their promotion with a 3-1 home win over Portsmouth, confining Charlton and Middlesbrough to the playoffs.

Alex Ferguson takes his 4th manager award of the season, whilst Walter smith scoops his 3rd following their league title success. Luis Aragones takes it for the second month running in Spain as his Real Betis side reach the Cup Winners Cup final.

May

May is the most pivotal month of the season, with various cups, leagues, promotions, relegations and playoffs to be decided across the globe. The football league in England has just two fixtures remaining, and as it's May bank holiday, everything will be decided by Monday.

Firstly though, the Premier League fixtures kick off the weekend and there's cause for the shock result graphic. Arsenal are thumped 3-0 by Sheffield Wednesday, which is a bad result no matter which way you look at it but more importantly, it hands Manchester United the title. In truth, the damage was done early on when Fergie's men won thirteen in a row, and Arsenal were never able to claw that gap back. Petter Rudi was the hero in The Owls' Highbury win, scoring twice and making the other. It's as you were at the bottom, with none of the bottom three managing a win. West Ham win at Elland Road in the clash of the two sides desperately trying to keep their heads above water. It's yet another Old Firm clash in Scotland, Rangers winning the latest chapter 1-0 thanks to Marco Negri. It's definitely been Rangers' year in Scotland. In Spain, Real Madrid keep up the pressure on Barcelona with a 4-0 win at 3rd placed Betis. The Catalans are getting nervy and need to come from behind to beat Real Oviedo, Sonny Anderson scoring yet again.

The May bank holiday fixtures are still a tradition back in 1998, though Newcastle will wish they weren't as they suffer a 1-0 loss at Bolton. With Leeds losing at

Chelsea, it means Bolton have given themselves a lifeline going into the final game of the season. Of course, in reality Bolton were relegated on the final day as Everton survived, so they'll be hoping for a different result this time as they travel to Villa Park. It's the end of the road for Leicester though, relegated after 2 seasons back in the top flight. Sunderland secure the First Division title with a win at Bradford, which will surely cheer up Peter Reid. The playoff places are also settled, with real life winners Charlton set to do battle with Middlesbrough (who came 6th), whilst it'll be an all Midlands affair when WBA take on Birmingham.

The First Division says goodbye to Bury, Tranmere and Portsmouth, all relegated with games to spare. They'll be replaced by Fulham & Watford, Graham Taylor rolling back the years to try and restore Watford to their former glory. Oldham, Wigan, York & Walsall will vie to be the third promoted team via the playoffs. Bristol Rovers & Wycombe are relegated comfortably, but the last two places are less clear cut. Milwall, Bournemouth & Carlisle all finish on forty four points, but Carlisle somehow survive despite having the worst goal difference of the three, shipping a mighty ninety five goals. This is because until 1999, the number of goals scored were the decider in the football league. The Third Division is won by Hull, player-managed by former England striker Mark Hateley. Exeter & Peterborough join Hull in the automatic slots, leaving Notts County (the real life champions), Darlington, Hartlepool& Colchester to scrap it out in the playoffs. Doncaster prop up the table with just twenty eight points and one hundred and one goals conceded –

Scarborough manage just a solitary point more and ship an impressive one hundred and seven goals, which is some effort.

Metz win the UEFA Cup, their all French final with Bordeaux is a 0-0 snooze fest for one hundred and twenty minutes and it needs penalties to separate them. Despite Bordeaux having legends such as Papin, Ricardinho and...Kiki Musampa, it's Metz who hold their nerve with Rigobert Song amongst the scorers. Song would go on to play for Liverpool & West Ham in the Premier League. Speaking of Liverpool, they draw their game in hand 1-1 with Manchester United to move them up to 8th. It's an odd looking table, with Blackburn, Wimbledon & Sheffield Wednesday all tied on sixty points just a point ahead of Liverpool, meaning the battle for European places will be a big story on the final day. Newcastle secure third with a win at Barnsley.

The final day of the season is here! The Premier League shares the stage with the first leg of the playoff semi-finals, with the pick of the results being Charlton's 2-1 win at Middlesbrough. It's all over Bolton though, beaten 2-0 at Aston Villa. First half goals from Dwight Yorke & Savo Milosevic condemn the Trotters to First Division football. We are denied a class finale due to Man Utd's ruthlessness, as the last day sees them travel to Arsenal in what could have been a title decider. Instead, Man Utd win a meaningless match 1-0 thanks to Paul Scholes' 34th goal of the season. For those wondering, Sol Campbell has played once since joining, and Patrick Andersson is yet to make his debut. Ronny

Johnsen is the star man, apparently. Wimbledon beat Liverpool 2-0 to secure 5th and deny Liverpool any European football, which is unthinkable. Chelsea are the big winners, climbing from 9th to 6th with a win over West Ham, taking advantage of losses for Blackburn, Sheff Wed & the aforementioned Liverpool result. It's also the final day in the Scottish Premier League, with Celtic & Rangers drawing their games. Dunfermline are relegated, whilst St. Johnstone will playoff with St. Mirren – the second last team in the Scottish Premier League taken on the runners up in Scottish Division One. There's still four games to go in Spain, where Barcelona continue to hold a four point advantage over Real Madrid. Celta Vigo are the first team to be relegated though, with just twenty three points from thirty five games played.

Midweek sees Sparta Prague win the Cup Winners Cup. I don't think anybody saw that coming. They win 2-1 against Betis in the Stadio Olimpico. I'm struggling to even come up with an anecdote about Sparta Prague, the only player of theirs I know is Horst Seigl but even he missed the game injured. Let's move on. Middlesbrough make a fool of me, beating Charlton 2-0 at the Valley to book a trip to Wembley. They'll face WBA, who knock out Birmingham 3-2 on aggregate with a late winner at St Andrews. Mayhem in that away end. Walsall light up the Division Two playoffs, after trailing 4-2 on aggregate with thirteen minutes to go, the Saddlers fight back to stun Oldham with three late goals to advance 5-4. Andy 'Unbelievable Tekkers' Ansah is part of their squad. York need extra time to see off Wigan but a win is a win, and York vs Walsall will be a great game for the neutral. Speaking of which, Darlington & Hartlepool draw 0-0 meaning Hartlepool advance-0 on aggregate, no doubt to the delight of Jeff Stelling. Colchester beat Notts County 3-2 on aggregate to round off the play offs, for now. Barcelona and Real Madrid both win, yet again, so it's a four point gap with three to play.

Terry Fenwick quits Portsmouth in disgust at their relegation to Division Two. Fenwick was capped twenty times by England so it's fair to say it's not the level he was used to. Another former England player, Alan Smith (now of *Sky Sports* fame) quits Scarborough. Given their defensive record, they might be better off appointing a defender. To round off the midweek news, St. Johnstone beat St Mirren 3-1 at home in the first leg of the relegation/promotion playoff.

Would you believe it, Newcastle United have won a trophy! A 1-0 triumph over newly promoted Manchester City seals the FA Cup for Kenny Dalglish, with stand-in striker Steve Watson scoring the all-important goal – Alan Shearer is out injured but should be back for the World Cup. Stuart Pearce lifts the trophy as I ponder whether Dalglish was the right man after all – maybe if Newcastle had faced a First Division team in the real 1998 final rather than the Premier League champions, it would all be much different. Stuart Pearce lifts the trophy for the Magpies. There's also a full round of games in Spain, where, shock horror, both Barcelona & Real Madrid win.

Don't think I've forgotten the Scottish FA Cup, because I haven't. It just takes place on the Sunday. Premier League Dundee Utd are beaten 2-0 by Division Two Livingston, which sums up a rather odd cup all round. Livingston have gained promotion to Division One by finishing 2nd, but it's quite another thing to win the FA Cup. They are managed by Jim Leishman, who is apparently now a Scottish Labour party Councillor.

Wednesday 20th May 1998 is a significant day – not only is it my tenth birthday, it's also an unbelievable night in the Bernabeu for Manchester United. The Champions League final with Juventus is going as you might expect when Daniel Fonesca slots past Kevin Pilkington (urgh) to give Juve a half time lead, but Teddy Sheringham equalises with twenty minutes to go before Scholes scores a stoppage time winner. After the madness, Dion Dublin lifts the trophy, which I'm sure Roy Keane was delighted about. It means my England lads will be in fine spirits, and I might call up Pilkington as some sort of good luck charm. I'm serious. Barcelona win away at Athletic Bilbao and Real Madrid smash Compostela 5-0 in the Bernabeu...hang on. A slight flaw then, two games in the same stadium on the same night, let's call it a quirk. As this was the penultimate game though, it means Barcelona are crowned champions. Oh and St. Johnstone draw with St Mirren to secure their spot as a Premier League side.

The last day of the Spanish League season has nothing riding on it at the top, but there's lots to play for at the bottom with only Celta Vigo actually relegated. Mallorca are next to go, thrashed at home by a rampant

Real Madrid. Merida also can't escape the trap door, a 0-0 draw at home to Real Oviedo sends them packing. That point for Real Oviedo is a vital one for them too, as Real Zaragoza's 4-1 loss at Real Sociedad keeps them up and sends Zaragoza to a life in the Segunda Division. I've criminally overlooked the Segunda throughout this book, but Logrones have won it and they'll be joined in the promotion party by Las Palmas, Rayo Vallecano & Extremadura – who are managed by Rafa Benitez. That is a fact.

The playoff finals are a time for celebration for Mr Stelling, a 2-0 win over Colchester gets the playoff weekend underway. The Division Two final belongs to Roger Boli, who scores four in a 5-0 win for Walsall against York. Just before the Division One playoff, the game does the old "shortlisting" thing which lists every team in order of ability (I think, though I can find no evidence of this) in their team colours. On a modern laptop this takes a couple of minutes but it was a ten minute marathon back in the day. Back from that though and it's Boro who are promoted, winning on penalties against WBA after a 1-1 draw. Paul Merson actually missed the "match point" but Gianluca Festa got him out of jail after matt carbon missed for WBA. WBA do have Matthew Le Tissier, who for some reason made the decision to drop down a division back in March, despite playing regularly for Southampton. It was such a news story it didn't even make a headline, so apologies to all Le Tissier fans out there.

The final domestic action comes in Spain, as Atletico Madrid spring a surprise by beating Barcelona 2-0 to win the Copa del Rey. Nobody in Barcelona's star studded side plays above a seven and it's even brought out the shock defeat headline. Kiko scores twice for Atletico – a reminder of the massive strength in depth Spain have.

I'm invited to name my twenty-five-man England squad for the World Cup Finals, which seems like a good time to end the chapter. Firstly though, the final Manager of the Month's of the season are here – and they go to all the league winners. Ferguson, Smith, Van Gaal. It's the same throughout all the other divisions, a total token award.

World Cup
Yes it's such a big deal we're going into our own little World Cup zone here.

My squad has been largely unchanged throughout, and as I'm oddly allowed to have twenty five rather than twenty three, that makes it even easier. Paul Merson is out, he hasn't been brilliant in the First Division or any of the games I've played him so I've gone for Darren Anderton. A wiser man than me would have picked him in the friendlies but he's always injured. Always. Paul Ince is also in, I might need to shore it up in some difficult games. Finally, that troublesome third goalkeeper spot has gone to Kevin Pilkington. Is he the third best keeper? No, of course he's not, but he's just won the Premier League and Champions League, playing a nine in the final, so he's coming as a good luck charm. I think I'm taking this Glenn Hoddle name too literally.

First up though it's a friendly away in Portugal, where I've decided to play pretty much my strongest team. That means Shearer up front with Scholes and Seaman in goal. It's a tight game which is 0-0 for ninety minutes, only for Gary Neville to head in a corner in injury time to give us a morale boosting win. The most realistic game in the World. Mind you, Portugal haven't even qualified for the World Cup, so perhaps not as good a result as it looks. They are a long way short of having a Cristiano Ronaldo type figure anyway.

One more friendly to go then, and it's rather laughably against Denmark, who'll we play in our World Cup opener 8 days later. Sack the fixture scheduler. I've given serious thought to cancelling it but instead, seeing as it's at Wembley, Pilko can make his debut and we'll have a good time. Shearer scores in a 1-0 win. For those wondering, in Schmeichel's absence Denmark have given the gloves to the pyjama wearing Burnley legend Brian 'the beast' Jensen, who right now is a twenty five year old at AZ Alkmaar. Typically, he got man of the match here after a string of saves. Pilko played an eight. In bad news, Steve McManaman was stretchered off with a foot injury. Hopefully he'll be back in time for the World Cup or I might have to get Paul Merson off his bender.

McManaman is out for a month, meaning he'd be back for the final at best. As if we'll get that far. It is apparently too late to replace him, which I find staggering given the tournament hasn't even started.

Barcelona sign Kiko in an act of petty revenge for a cool £11.25m.

Michael Owen is ruled out for two weeks. He'll miss at least two group games, which is a shame. Owen started the season on fire but lost his place in the Liverpool team to Karl Heinz Riedle, so he's pretty much in reverse to real life. Owen burst onto the scene in the 1997/98 season and was given his debut by Glenn Hoddle in a friendly against Chile, and of course went on to score a great individual goal in the World Cup. Basically, he arrived in the tournament as a hot commodity. Here, his season has fizzled out.

With no more injury disaster's to report, we've arrived at the eve of the tournament. World Cup 1998 was a great time to be a football fan – the first tournament with thirty two teams, kick off times perfect for a European audience and *Vindaloo* on the radio. If you thought *Three Lions 98* was the only anthem of the time, think again. *Vindaloo* was the unofficial anthem of that summer, mainly because it was so much more likeable than England's official song *(How does it feel to be) On Top of the World?*by England United, which included the Spice Girls to give you some indication of the direction this one went. Without dwelling on this for too long, it was booed when played at Wembley. Anyway, music aside, it's time for the football to get underway. As was tradition at the time, the holders start things off and that means Brazil, who thrash Mexico 3-0. With the in form Sonny Anderson partnering Ronaldo, Brazil will take some stopping. The other cannon fodder in this group are Yugoslavia and Belgium, who draw 0-0.

Group B, have a word with yourselves. The hosts France can't find a way past Brad Friedel, who gets man of the match as the USA take a creditable 0-0 draw. It's a similar story in the other game in Group B, where Norway find Mark Bosnich in inspired form and that too ends 0-0. Four games, three 0-0 draws. Such a great advert for the game.

Goals! In the game everybody is talking about, Tunisia beat Saudi Arabia 2-1. The Saudis miss a pen too, a classic by the standard we've seen so far. Spain follow that up by beating Bulgaria 1-0, meaning Group C has seen two winners and goals in both games, a remarkable achievement.

Nigeria actually have the better of Russia to kick off Group D, but it is the Russians who steal a 1-0 win. Morocco and Cameroon complete the group – meaning we have three African teams in the group – but they draw 0-0 as it's been a while.

The Dutch are in Group E, and all of their talent eventually pays off as they score two late goals to beat South Africa 2-0. Switzerland and Paraguay are also found here, but they draw 1-1 to shoot each other in the proverbial foot.

Group F sees a huge clash between Italy and Argentina, which the Italians steal with a late Enrico Chiesa goal. Fabrizio Ravanelli had opened the scoring before

Argentina struck back immediately. Colombia are also in this group, with the unmistakable hair of Carlos Valderrama in the middle of the park and Tino Asprilla leading the line. They see off China 2-0, with Valderrama rounding off a comfortable win where China didn't manage a single shot.

Forget about Group G, the scheduling means they have to wait one more day and it's time for England vs. Denmark (and this time, it's for real)

England vs Denmark – World Cup Group H – As it happened

Welcome to Felix Bollaert, Nord for England's first game in the 1998 World Cup. If we're being pedantic, it's the first World Cup game England have played for eight years since losing to West Germany in the 1990 Semi-finals, but the less we are reminded of that the better. Denmark are England's opponents, and the two sides bizarrely played a friendly at Wembley earlier this month. The Danes have four Jensen's, three Andersen's and two Laudrup's, but England only have one aim tonight – and that is three points.

The other teams in the group, Chile and Romania, are also playing following this match, so by ten pm tonight we'll have a good idea if England are on course to qualify from this group.

First though, let's get some team news.

England bring in Darren Anderton for the injured Steve McManaman, but otherwise it's their usual team. David Seaman is in goal and Tony Adams is captain.
England: Seaman, G Neville, P Neville, Adams (c), Dublin, Campbell, Beckham, Gascoigne, Anderton, Shearer, Scholes. **Subs:** Pilkington, Eadie, R Ferdinand, Fowler, Sheringham.

Denmark have a full squad to choose from but they were dealt a huge blow earlier in the year when Peter Schmeichel was ruled out of the tournament. AZ Goalkeeper Brian Jensen has picked up the gloves in his absence.
Denmark: Br Jensen, J Jensen, B Jensen, Heintze, Anderson, Helveg, Tomasson, B Laudrup, Nielsen (c), Andersen, M Laudrup **Subs:** Christensen, Larsen, JF Jensen, Gronkjaer, Jepsen

Remarkably, Denmark have two players called Brian Jensen. Anyway, whilst we brought you the team news, the anthems have been sang and it's time for kick off. Here we go!

KICK OFF England get us underway in Group H.

2 Minutes – GOAL FOR ENGLAND! England 1 – 0 Denmark (Alan Shearer)

Shearer certain to score! David Beckham is the architect, putting in an irresistible cross that England number 9 Alan Shearer thrives on. He meets the cross with a bullet header and one of the Brian Jensen's is left with no chance. England have lift off!

11 Minutes – Close from Denmark as Soren Andersen picks up Brian Laudrup's pass and drills a shot just wide of Seaman's post.

15 Minutes – Close again! This time Nielsen is the provider for Andersen but again the Vicenza striker is off target. Worrying for England though

19 Minutes – England! Sort yourselves out. Andersen has his third chance of the match, and he manages to get this one on target. It's straight at Seaman though and England survive.

23 Minutes – Shearer for 2-0! No! Jensen makes a great save to deny Shearer's far post header, and Scholes meets Gascoigne's resulting corner but Jensen saves that too.

29 Minutes – Soren Andersen will have a sleepless night. He tries two efforts in a minute, the first he pokes wide and the second is a speculative one from fully thirty yards that Tony Adams charges down.

33 Minutes – Anderton puts Shearer in and from a tight angle, the England striker smashes the ball at goal but Jensen paws it away. Gary Neville heads over the resulting corner.

38 Minutes – Shearer's fourth effort of the match brings another save from Jensen, this time Scholes slides Shearer in but he can't beat Jensen.

44 Minutes – Half time is close but there's still time for Gary Neville to head over when unmarked from a corner.

HALF TIME – England 1 – 0 Denmark

Catch your breath, make a cuppa, and re-join us in fifteen minutes for more of the same. So far so good for England though.

England have had 8 shots to Denmark's five, the stats reflect the score line really. All of Denmark's shots have come from Soren Andersen, whilst Shearer has had four shots and all four have hit the target for England, with the all important one coming in the second minute.

KICK OFF – Denmark get the second half underway

46 Minutes – Guess what? Andersen shoots wide. six shots, two on target. No goals yet.

49 Minutes – **GOAL! England 2 – 0 Denmark (Alan Shearer)**
That old familiar celebration is out again as Shearer nets his third goal in a month against Denmark and his second of the night. Gascoigne finds Shearer who works himself half a yard and picks his spot in the far corner to finally beat Jensen for a second time.

52 Minutes – **GOAL! England 3 – 0 Denmark (Alan Shearer – Hat trick)**

A World Cup hat trick! Scholes is the provider this time, playing Shearer in behind after the Danes get the offside trap all wrong. Shearer waits for Jensen to commit before chipping it over him. The arm is in the air, the match ball will soon be in his possession.

54 Minutes – **GOAL! England 3 – 1 Denmark (Soren Andersen)**

Hold the phone, Andersen has finally scored. It's his seventh shot and he finds the corner as though he's never missed a chance in his life. Denmark back in it with plenty of time on the clock.

56 Minutes – **SUBSTITUTION**

Change for Denmark as captain Peter Nielsen is replaced by John Faxe Jensen, formerly of Arsenal.

61 Minutes – Chaos from a Denmark corner sees Michael Laudrup have a shot parried and Brian Jensen (the defender) sees his follow up shot somehow kept out by Seaman. Fine goalkeeping!

65 Minutes – Shearer at it again, Jensen saves this time though. The resulting corner falls to Gary Neville, who has somehow managed five shots today. This one is the first on target but Jensen is equal to it.

72 Minutes – Some big pressure from Denmark and a couple of quick fire chances. Firstly Brian Laudrup feeds Andersen who sees his shot tipped over by Seaman. The resulting corner falls to Tomasson, who gets a good connection on the shot but it's deflected over.

73 Minutes – **SUBSTITUTION**
Time for experienced heads, off comes Paul Scholes and
on comes Teddy Sheringham.

75 Minutes – **GOAL FOR ENGLAND! England 4 – 1
Denmark (Paul Gascoigne)**
Sheringham has only been on the pitch two minutes but
moments after he should score, he sets up Paul
Gascoigne who seals this win. It's fitting that the only
man on the pitch tonight who played that faithful night
in 1990 has scored and hopefully banished his demons
of that night.

76 Minutes – **SUBSTITUTION**
With the game safe, England sub Shearer & Beckham
for Fowler & Eadie.

80 Minutes – **YELLOW CARD**
Jann Jensen goes in the book for an untidy challenge on
Darren Anderton.

82 Minutes – **GOAL FOR ENGLAND! England 5 – 1
Denmark (Robbie Fowler)**
Good grief, England have gone mad. Gary Neville
marauds up the right wing and pulls the ball back for
Robbie Fowler, who doesn't miss from ten yards. If
England ever post a more significant 5-1 win in my
lifetime, I'll start a blog about a video game that's
nearly twenty years old.

83 Minutes – **SUBSTITUTION**

The game is finally up for Denmark, who are already turning their attention to game two. Brian Laudrup is given a rest for Allan Jepsen of Hamburg.

84 Minutes – **GOAL FOR ENGLAND! England 6 – 1 Denmark (Robbie Fowler)**

Six of the best! The two substitutes combine, Sheringham plays in Fowler and on his left foot, you know the result. Brian Jensen looks livid. The goalkeeper that is, the centre half looks fairly bemused.

88 Minutes – Alan Shearer is announced as man of the match for his hat trick. 40,998 people have witnessed this. The England contingent are singing the National Anthem.

90 Minutes – **GOAL FOR ENGLAND! England 7 – 1 Denmark (Robbie Fowler – Hat trick)**

Oh stop it. You're spoiling us now. Gascoigne's corner is whipped in, Robbie Fowler really wants a hat trick and he meets it with the perfect header. 7-1 – but who will take the match ball home?

FULL TIME – England 7 – 1 Denmark

You couldn't make it up. A tournament shy of goals and it's England who provide the entertainment. The 1992 European Champions have been dispatched.
Join us next time for England vs Chile, but we can't promise more of the same.

That result means we're at least on course to replicate England's performance in the real world, after they started their campaign with a 2-0 success against Tunisia. It's Chile up next for me though.

The other game in Group H sees Romania come from behind to beat Chile – the evergreen Gheorghe Hagi score the winner three minutes from the end. Romania got through their group with England in real life and celebrated by dyeing their hair blonde. They looked silly. They're on course to do the same thing here though, I imagine they'll put up more of a fight than Denmark did when we meet them.

Finally, it is the turn of Group G. The Germans are the undisputable favourites to advance from this group, underlined by a comfortable 2-0 win over their likely closest challengers Sweden. Klinsmann scores both goals, to add to his fifteen goals and twenty-one assists he got at club level – he's thirty four next month! Japan beat Jamaica 1-0 in the other game – the Reggae Boys can boast Robbie Earle as a star player, to give you some idea of the task they face.

Disaster in the England camp! Gascoigne has a damaged foot and will be out for two weeks. That almost translates to end of tournament, the last thing Gazza needs after Italia 90. Now I have to decide whether to replace him like for like or change the formation entirely, he really is pivotal in that central midfield role.

Back in Group A, one team who have no trouble with depth is Brazil who put five past Yugoslavia. Ronaldo gets one but the star of the show is midfielder Rai, who scores four. Ronaldo also missed a late penalty as he bids to underline his status as the best striker in the world. That result coupled with Mexico beating Belgium 2-1 puts the holders through with minimal fuss. Gilles de Bilde scores for Belgium, as I break into the *Bob the Builder* chant that accompanied his career in England.

After four games in Group B, there has been one goal. France are basically throwing a massive party and then got the Monopoly board out, but Florian Maurice gets them out of jail free with a late winner against Norway. The USA and Australia draw 0-0, but to be honest back in 1998 I don't imagine if either country will have been all too bothered. France, with one goal and four points, top the group. Sacre Bleu.

Spain keep their 100% record with a comfortable win over Tunisia. With Bulgaria beating Saudi Arabia 1-0, the Spanish are through with a game to spare, to the surprise of nobody. Big news back home though as Manchester United buy Steve Watson from Newcastle for £4m plus Grant Brebner. Right. Michael Owen has recovered too, but unless he fancies playing central midfield that is no use to me.

Group D is an odd group, there's no obvious winner and three African nations. Russia complete the group and are flying when former Man Utd & Everton hero Andrei Kanchelskis puts them 2-0 up, only for the plucky Moroccans to claw it back to 2-2. Finidi George, who will grace Portman Road in years to come, scores the winner as Nigeria beat Cameroon to move up to 2nd.

Holland are the latest team to advance with a game to spare, their 2-1 defeat of Switzerland sealing their last sixteen spot. Patrick Kluivert, who is about to turn twenty two, scores both goals and takes his International record to eight goals in thirteen games, which isn't too shabby at all. South Africa draw 0-0 with Paraguay as the fight to finish 2nd doesn't heat up. There's also a surprise Group H fixture (my group), as Denmark come from behind to beat Romania. Hagi gave Romania a half time lead but the Laudrup brothers each netted in the second half to throw the group wide open. In many ways I would have preferred Romania to win to take Denmark out of the equation. We'll just have to beat Chile to ensure that is still the case.

Group F continues to go to form, though China nearly cause a major upset against Argentina. A 40th minute equaliser from Qun Wei looks like it will be enough for a famous point for China until Real Madrid's Fernando Redondo scores a late winner. Italy dominate against Colombia but can only manage one goal, Antonio Conte's first half goal earns them a second win and a place in round two.

It's that time again though, can we make it two wins out of two and all but secure our second round place?

World Cup Group H – England vs Chile – As it happened

Welcome back to our coverage of England's World Cup games. Today, England take on Chile in Parc des Princes. As the team's line up for the National Anthems, here's today's team news.

England are forced into one change, the injured Paul Gascoigne replaced by Robbie Fowler. The England manager could not resist playing Fowler from the start after his hat-trick from the bench last time out. It means a slight change in formation, a more attacking shape with Scholes in behind Shearer & Fowler, with Anderton and Beckham in midfield.

England: Seaman, G Neville, P Neville, Dublin, Adams (c), Campbell, Beckham, Anderton, Scholes, Fowler, Shearer. **Subs:** Pilkington, R Ferdinand, Butt, Eadie, Sheringham

Chile are without the injured Clarence Acuna and Miguel Ramirez, but star men Marcelo Salas & Ivan Zamorano will be sure to give England a tough night. **Chile:** Ramirez, Castaneda, Mendoza, Margas, Rojas, Sierra, Barrera, Valencia, Zamorano, Basay, Salas **Subs:** Ruiz, Vergara, Reyes, Osorio, Vega
With the anthems done and the players shaking hands, let's get this show on the road.

KICK OFF – England kick us underway

2 Minutes – **YELLOW CARD**
An early problem here for England, as Salas easily beats Dion Dublin and the former Coventry man cynically takes Salas down. Yellow for Dublin, but more worryingly a dangerous free kick for Chile.

3 Minutes – **GOAL FOR CHILE! England 0 – 1 Chile (Ivan Zamorano)**

Oh, England. It's a reversal of the Denmark game as their opponents strike first. Salas' free kick is met by Rojas, Seaman can only parry the shot and Zamorano reacts first to gleefully give his side the lead. Disaster.

8 Minutes – First sight of goal for England as Tony Adams meets Beckham's corner but it goes inches over the bar.

14 Minutes – Close for England, and again it's from a Beckham set piece. This time his free kick is met by the diminutive Paul Scholes but he heads just over.

18 Minutes – **YELLOW CARD**
Gary Neville joins Dublin in the book for a pull back on Basay. This time though Salas' free kick is blasted over the bar by Sierra on the turn.

21 Minutes – **RED CARD – CHILE (Gabriel Mendoza)**
Is this the game changer? Scholes tries to thread Shearer in behind but Gabriel Mendoza sticks out his right hand and pats the ball away. The referee deems him to have stopped a goal scoring opportunity and it's a red card. Huge lifeline for England.

27 Minutes – Half chance for England. Shearer feeding Fowler inside the box but he is off balance and the ball flies over the bar. England yet to hit the target.

29 Minutes – **GOAL FOR ENGLAND! England 1 – 1 Chile (Darren Anderton)**
England are level! Pick the bones out of this one though. It's great work from Robbie Fowler, who beats

his man down the left of the box and hangs a ball up to the back post. Alan Shearer attacks it as you would expect and the ball hits the goalkeeper – you couldn't really call it a save – and the ball rebounds to Phil Neville, of all people. Neville junior shows all the finishing technique you would expect of a man with one career goal and his effort is parried by the goalkeeper, with the ball arriving at the feet of Darren Anderton. Anderton is the coolest man in the Parc des Princes and slots the ball into the open goal to send the England fans crazy. Get in!

34 Minutes – **YELLOW CARD**
Role reversal here as Salas fouls Dublin well after the ball has gone – easy yellow card for the Chilean.

37 Minutes – **YELLOW CARD**
Chile goalkeeper and captain Marcelo Ramirez has had a lot to say since his team mate was sent off, and it turns out he has said too much and is booked. Tempers are flaring.

41 Minutes – **GOAL FOR CHILE!England 1 – 2 Chile (Marcelo Salas)**
This wasn't in the script. Chile win a corner and it is again met by Rojas, again Seaman can't hold on and this time Marcelo Salas is the benefactor, lashing in the loose ball. ten men or not, England have a mountain to climb to turn this around.

44 Minutes – Late chance for England but Adams heads Beckham's free kick wide.

HALF TIME – England 1 – 2 Chile

An all-action half but not a good one for England, who have lacked inspiration in Gascoigne's absence. Chile are bound to put everybody behind the ball in the second half to make it as difficult as possible for England to get back into the game.

England have had seven shots to Chile's five and have just about shaded the half, but Chile were reduced to ten men from the 21st minute. It should be an interesting second half.

KICK OFF – Chile get us back under way, no changes for either team.

46 Minutes – Salas tries one from way out that nearly catches David Seaman unaware, but the Arsenal man gets across to tip it away. Tony Adams deals with the corner.

48 Minutes – **GOAL FOR ENGLAND! England 2 – 2 Chile (Alan Shearer)**

The hand is in the air! Paul Scholes plays a beautiful pass in behind Chile's defence and Shearer does not miss one on one with the goalkeeper (usually). It's four for the tournament for Shearer but more importantly, England are back on terms.

54 Minutes – Heavy England pressure now. Firstly Anderton heads a corner wide and shortly afterwards, Robbie Fowler's shot is only parried by the goalkeeper, but it is a Chilean body first to the rebound.

58 Minutes – Robbie Fowler, it's not your day. After everything he touched went to gold last time out, it's been a disaster of a night so far for the Liverpool frontman. Here he wastes a good opportunity by shooting about twenty yards wide.

63 Minutes – **YELLOW CARD**
Ivan Zamorano is the latest in the book, this time for a foul on Alan Shearer.

65 Minutes – **GOAL FOR ENGLAND! England 3 – 2 Chile (Tony Adams)**
The captain has done it! A free kick isn't properly cleared and the ball drops to Tony Adams, who finishes like a striker (well, like Shearer as opposed to Fowler) and it's 3-2!

67 Minutes – **RED CARD**
Good grief. Robbie Fowler is in behind and Javier Margas panics. Margas, who displays the kind of skills that encouraged West Ham to sign him in reality, chops Fowler down and is given his marching orders. Chile down to nine men.

71 Minutes – Beckham is the latest to try his luck, but it's straight at the goal keeper. England need to kill this off quickly.

74 Minutes – **SUBSTITUTION**
Robbie Fowler's strange old evening is over, with Teddy Sheringham on in his place.

80 Minutes – Crossbar! Yet another Chile set piece causes mayhem, Zamorano meets it with a bullet header but it crashes off the crossbar and David Seaman gathers the loose ball. Huge let off for England.

83 Minutes – **YELLOW CARD**
Esteban Valencia becomes the fourth Chilean in the book, kicking a lump out of David Beckham.

86 Minutes – Oh, Teddy. A great chance to seal the win goes begging when Sheringham can only shoot straight at Ramirez. It's the Chilean keeper's 7th save of the night.

87 Minutes – **SUBSTITUTION**
David Beckham is off and Nicky Butt is on as England try to hold on to what they've got.

FULL TIME – England 3 – 2 Chile
Massive relief greets the full time whistle, that was a huge battle for England. Not just metaphorically but also physically. It's two out of two for England, six points and a place in the last sixteen almost guaranteed.

It's not all good news, as Gary Neville collected his second yellow card of the tournament and will miss the final game against Romania. Le Saux will probably come in with Phil Neville switching sides. We'll see though. McManaman is still a week away whilst Gascoigne is no nearer a return, worryingly.
Poor Japan are destroyed by Germany 5-0. Klinsmann scores twice more, he really is getting better with age. Sweden only beat Jamaica 1-0 but it is enough to end

the hopes of the Jamaicans, as Sweden and Japan each have three points and face each other in the final game. Oddly enough, Henrik Larsson is only on Sweden's bench.

With just the final game to go in each group, we enter the heavy heights of four games in a day. Belgium and Brazil draw 1-1 in an odd game where Brazil have no shots on target but score via an own goal, only for Luc Nillis to equalise. Brazil were already through but two points sends Belgium out. Mexico edge past Yugoslavia 1-0 to take 2nd spot. If my calculations are right (they rarely are) I'll be up against this group in the last sixteen, so it's imperative we win the group. Goal shy group B bursts into action as France rack up a 2-0 win against Australia. The hosts will be joined by Norway in the last sixteen, as they beat the USA 1-0 to take second spot. Norway go through having scored one goal and conceded one goal.

Spain complete their rout of Group C, beating Saudi Arabia 2-0 to finish with a 100% record. Bulgaria draw with Tunisia and take 2nd spot by virtue of having lost to Spain by less of a margin, such is the mediocrity of this group. Group D is not much better, our old friend Hassan Kachloul equalises for Morocco against Nigeria but his side go out as the game finishes 1-1. Cameroon can go through with a win against Russia but despite equalising late on, it finishes 1-1 and Russia top the group with five points, ahead of Nigeria with four.

Argentina are out! Hopefully David Beckham finds Diego Simeone's face and laughs in it, he won't be winding up the English in this game. Their exit comes after a draw with Colombia, the World's hairiest man Valderrama scoring the equaliser that eliminates the Argentinians on goal difference. Basically, China's goal has knocked them out as they didn't score past Colombia. Italy 'thrash' China 1-0, having fifteen shots to China's 1 but only scoring an 80th minute winner through Massimo Crippa. That maintains Italy's 100% record. Another side with a perfect record is Holland, who defeat Paraguay 2-0 thanks to Ronald De Boer and Philip Cocu. They are joined in the last 16 by Switzerland, who see off South Africa 2-0.

Germany put just the four past Jamaica, they really are in a weak group though. Klinsmann only manages to net once. Sweden, as expected, take the 2nd spot with a 3-0 win over Japan. Everybody's favourite party animal Thomas Brolin nets the 3rd goal.

So that only leaves one group...
World Cup Group H – England vs Romania
7-1. 3-2. England are the new entertainers. A place in the last 16 is almost guaranteed, but a point is needed to avoid facing Brazil in the last sixteen. Romania will be tough opponents, as Ireland found out in qualifying, but England are riding the crest of a wave here and have a good chance of achieving their target tonight in Bordeaux.

Team News
There are two changes for **England**, with the suspended Gary Neville replaced by Graeme Le Saux and Teddy Sheringham starting ahead of Robbie Fowler. Steve McManaman and Paul Gascoigne have

delivered positive fitness news this week and might make the last sixteen match, should England make it.
England: Seaman, P Neville, Le Saux, Dublin, Adams (c), Campbell, Beckham, Anderton, Scholes, Sheringham, Shearer. **Subs:** Pilkington, Fowler, Eadie, R Ferdinand, Butt

Romania are missing Stanciu and Zotinca but have their strongest eleven available, including former Barcelona players Hagi and Popescu as well as Chelsea's Dan Petrescu.
Romania: Prunea, Rednic, Prodan, Mihali, Petrescu, Selymes, Lupescu, Galca, Popescu (c), Hagi, Lacatus.
Subs: Ilie, Tene, Raducioiu, Pana, Sabau

KICK OFF – The anthems have been belted out – Romania kick us underway

5 Minutes – A timid start but the first half chance falls to Phil Neville. Unfortunately, he is pretty much the last person you want a chance to fall to, and he heads David Beckham's corner well wide.

1 Minutes – **YELLOW CARD**
Steady Teddy. A late tackle by Teddy Sheringham as he tries to stop Mircea Rednic making a clearance results in a yellow card. And rightly so.

18 Minutes – Chance for Romania as Selymes meets Petrescu's corner but Tony Adams makes a big block to keep it goalless. Very tight game so far.

25 Minutes – Dion! What are you doing!? The big man lets a long ball drop over his head and he is chased down by Gheorghe Popescu, who sticks a boot out and nearly catches David Seaman off his line, but it drifts just wide. Dublin looks relieved.

31 Minutes – Calm down Phil Neville. His second shot of the game is marginally closer than the first, but still not quite close enough to trouble Florian Prunea.

36 Minutes – **YELLOW CARD**
Alan Shearer is in the book for blocking a Romanian pass with his hand. The ref deemed it to be deliberate and to be fair, Shearer has few complaints.

42 Minutes – Sitter! Oh Graeme Le Saux, what are you thinking!? Beckham swings the corner in to the near post and Sheringham has got ahead of his marker, flinging a right boot at the ball. Prunea pulls off a great reaction save but the ball drops loose for Le Saux who must score – but he doesn't. It goes way over the bar off his shin and that's a golden chance.

HALF TIME – Romania 0 – 0 England
You will struggle to see a duller game than this. Romania trying to bring England on to them, England happy with a point. It's cat and mouse except the cat doesn't need to eat. Yet.
The stats show it to be a fairly even game in terms of possession, with England managing four shots to Romania's two. Romania are yet to test David Seaman whilst England have just that one effort on target from Teddy Sheringham on the stroke of half time.

KICK OFF – England get the second half underway.

47 Minutes – **YELLOW CARD**
David Beckham holds back Rednic and he joins Shearer and Sheringham in the book.

53 Minutes – Anderton! Wide. Scholes takes aim from just outside the box, a real cracker of a strike but it hits the crossbar. Darren Anderton follows in but shows no composure and blasts the ball over the bar.

59 Minutes – A rare Romanian attack sees Marius Lacatus go on a little run before trying to chip David Seaman. He nearly manages it as well, but Seaman recovers to tip the shot over for a corner. Petrescu's delivery causes yet more mayhem, but Tony Adams stands strong to block Rednic's header.

62 Minutes – Finally England have created something. It's a small step, with Sheringham feeding Shearer but his strike is blocked on the way through. The resulting corner is headed straight at the keeper by Sheringham.

65 Minutes – **SUBSTITUTION**
England are the first to blink, taking off Paul Scholes and bringing on Darren Eadie. Scholes has done admirably well in a more withdrawn mode but it's not his game.

71 Minutes – **YELLOW CARD**
Dion Dublin is the next in the book for a foul on Tibor Selymes. That's four England players in the book now.

75 Minutes – Did that clip the crossbar? Shearer let's fly from fully thirty yards and it dips dramatically and drops just over the bar – replays show it just clipped the crossbar.

78 Minutes - Shearer puts Sheringham in one on one but Prunea is out quickly to save. It's fair to say Teddy's goose is cooked.

79 Minutes – **SUBSTITUTION**
With that, Robbie Fowler is on for Teddy Sheringham

86 Minutes – Darren Eadie has been neat and tidy since he came on, but this is a bit more adventurous as his shot from the edge of the box it's struck with venom but it is inches wide.

89 Minutes -Sol Campbell is named man of the match, which tells you all you need to know about this game.

FULL TIME – England 0 – 0 Romania
Well it wasn't pretty, but England got the point they needed. Romania will be very disappointed that they could barely lay a glove on England but it's job done for Glenn Hoddle (or the man pretending to be him)

Denmark beat Chile in the other game, two goals for Soren Andersen taking his tally to three remarkably. That means Denmark advance and the Romanian's are going home – no blonde hair dye this time.

With that, the last sixteen is set. I've already achieved what my real life counterpart couldn't and that is top the group to avoid the group winners in the last sixteen. As I predicted, it is Mexico we face whilst Denmark take on Brazil. If we beat Mexico, it'll be Germany (or Norway...) in the Quarters. There's a potential France vs Brazil quarter final, so there's no chance of a repeat of the real 1998 final.

Gascoigne is back! So does Steve McManaman. Great times for us at least. It's less good times for Denmark, who fresh from shipping seven to England lose 5-1 to Brazil. It's slightly less embarrassing to lose to the World Champions but Brian Jensen will curse the day Peter Schmeichel's pelvis shattered. Remarkably, Soren Andersen had briefly levelled for Denmark before Sonny Anderson and friends took over. France are through to face the Champions after a penalty shootout success against Sweden. The shootout followed another 0-0 draw for the most boring hosts ever, though Sweden missed all three of their penalties to surrender quite meekly in the end. The earlier good news is offset with the news that Beckham, Dublin & Sheringham have all reached their yellow card quota. That could have been announced earlier, surely!?Selection headache to come then.

Spain are the next team to book their last sixteen place, seeing off Colombia 3-1. Spain's form is very impressive and they will no doubt have been relieved to have been facing Colombia rather than Argentina. The draw is opening up nicely for them, as they'll next face Switzerland who need extra time to see of Russia, but

Stephane Chapuisat scores with ten minutes to go to see the Swiss through 1-0.

Gazza man! What are you playing at? He's only gone and bruised his jaw, presumably from drinking too much, and he's out for another week. With Beckham out already, this is getting absurd. The tournament progresses though, and it's another good day for the seeded teams who both record 2-0 wins. Holland see off Nigeria whilst Italy ease past Bulgaria. Not the most exciting day of World Cup action but tomorrow is the big day.

Here we go then, England vs Mexico with the winners to face Germany or Norway. This is the round where Glenn Hoddle's England were undone on penalties against Argentina – I'm very keen to avoid the same fate against potentially weaker opponents.

World Cup Last Sixteen – England vs Mexico – As it happened

It's do or die time for England, win or bust. We could be here all night if it takes extra time and penalties – which you wouldn't rule out. England posted an impressive win against Denmark but have failed to hit those heights ever since, particularly lacking creativity in the absence of Gascoigne and McManaman, whilst Mexico recovered from being beaten by Brazil in the tournament opener to record back to back wins. It's fascinatingly poised – who wants it more?

Team News

England are forced into three changes as David Beckham, Dion Dublin & Teddy Sheringham are all suspended. Rio Ferdinand, fit again Steve McManaman and Darren Eadie are the replacements. Gary Neville returns from his ban to take the place of Graeme Le Saux.

England: Seaman, G Neville, P Neville, Adams (c), R Ferdinand, Campbell, Anderton, McManaman, Eadie, Scholes, Shearer. **Subs:** Pilkington, Southgate, Wright, Fowler, Butt.

Mexico have no new injury problems but are still without centre half Juan Ramirez through injury.

Mexico: Campos, Suarez, Alves, Guttierez, Garcia Aspe, Hermosillo, Coyote, Vidrio, Ambriz, Espinosa, Garcia. **Subs:** M Campos, Navarro, Wanchope, Lightbourne, S Garcia.

Kick Off – Opening pleasantries exchanged, Mexico kick us underway at Parc Lescure

5 Minutes – Mexico are adopting similar tactics to Romania, trying to get England's beleaguered midfield to come on to them so they are ripe for a counter attack. Very little action so far.

11 Minutes – Finally, a chance! Shearer and Scholes combine and the Manchester United man gets a shot away but Campos tips it round. Good save! McManaman's corner is awful though.

18 Minutes – Scholes tries one from well outside the box but it lacks power and is easy for Campos to gather.

24 Minutes – Shearer is almost put through one on one with Campos but the ball is slightly over hit and the England man can only toe poke it off Campos.

30 Minutes – Goal FOR ENGLAND! England 1 – 0 Mexico (Darren Eadie)

England are in front! A corner is whipped over and Paul Scholes arrives with a trademark run. His shot hits the post but Darren Eadie is on hand to smash in the rebound. It's been hard work, but England lead!

33 Minutes – Mexico try to hit straight back, as Vidrio's corner is headed wide by Espinosa.

38 Minutes – Another chance for Espinosa, this time from open play. A whipped cross is a good height for the central midfielder but he gets it all wrong and it's way off target. Espinosa is without a club at present, and with a finish like that perhaps it is no surprise.

HALF TIME – England 1 – 0 Mexico

A very cagey first half then, with very little goalmouth action. The most important action saw Darren Eadie score his first England goal and give his side a lead which they'll look to build on in the second half.

A quick perusal of the stats show that England have managed five shots to Mexico's two, with the Mexicans yet to hit the target. By contrast, Campos has been tested four times although one of those was the goal from Eadie.

For years we've craved a left sided English player – could Eadie be it?

Kick Off – England get the second half underway.

46 Minutes – **GOAL FOR ENGLAND! England 2 – 0 Mexico (Darren Anderton)**
Oh you sleepy Mexicans. The second half is barely thirty seconds old when Phil Neville of all people heads a ball clear. The Mexicans leave it to each other and Anderton runs on to the loose ball and chips it over Campos. Game over? We hope so!

52 Minutes – Shearer wants a goal but this effort from fully thirty yards won't be it, as it whistles wide of Campos' goal.

60 Minutes – Gary Neville loves an effort these days, this time he collects the ball from Steve McManaman's free kick and drills a shot in but it's straight at Campos who makes a comfortable save.

63 Minutes – **YELLOW CARD**
Steve McManaman, who must be a candidate to be subbed on his first game back, puts in a clumsy challenge on Carlos Hermosillo and gets a deserved yellow card.

68 Minutes – Mexico aren't done here just yet. Missael Espinosa has their first effort on target, collecting a neat layoff and hitting a shot that Seaman does well to push away for a corner. The corner comes to nothing.

70 Minutes – **SUBSTITUTION**
As predicted, an exhausted looking Steve McManaman is withdrawn and Nicky Butt is on to shore things up.

73 Minutes – **GOAL FOR ENGLAND! England 3 – 0 Mexico (Alan Shearer)**
Game over! There will be no need for any jokes about Mexican stand offs. Phil Neville is the architect again, putting in a sumptuous ball to the back post where Alan Shearer meets it with a neat side foot volley that Campos can't get near. See you in the last eight.

74 Minutes – **SUBSTITUTION**
With the game in the bag and England wary of any more suspensions, Alan Shearer is withdrawn and Ian Wright will get his first minutes of the campaign.

80 Minutes – England are playing keep ball, the game is up now and they can turn their attention to that Quarter final tie with Germany or Norway.

83 Minutes – Crossbar! Nearly a consolation for Mexico, as centre half Luis Alberto Alves meets Vidrio's corner but his head smacks the crossbar and Seaman can claim it. When it's not your day...

86 Minutes – **YELLOW CARD**
Claudio Suarez is in the book for Mexico, pulling back Anderton.

SUBSTITUTION
Paul Scholes is given five minutes rest and Robbie Fowler is on.

88 Minutes – Man of the match is announced as Mexico's Jorge Campos. Well, of course.

FULL TIME – England 3 – 0 Mexico
England are through to the quarter finals! With nine shots to Mexico's four, they are deserved winners and the fact Campos got man of the match says it all. The three goal scorers plus the Neville brothers all play a rating of eight in what can only be described as a great team performance.

Oh my word, the Germans are out. Thomas Myhre of Everton withstands nineteen shots from the Germans but keeps a clean sheet and sends it to penalties. Myhre then saves from Klinsmann of all people and the dream is over. It'll be Norway vs England in the Quarter Finals. Funnily enough, Ole Gunnar Solskjaer signs for Chelsea in celebration.

So, the top half of the draw will see the Hosts France take on the holders Brazil, with the winners due to face Spain or Switzerland. The bottom half sees a box office clash between Holland and Italy, with England or Norway lying in wake.

We're getting serious now, as the repeat of the actual 1998 World Cup Final is filled with drama. It's looking comfortable for Brazil, who lead through Sonny Anderson, but it all kicks off in the 66th minute when goalkeeper Zetti is sent off for a professional foul on Florian Maurice, who slots away the penalty. It goes all the way to penalties as ten man Brazil battle hard, and things look to have swung back in the Champions favour when Maurice's penalty is saved by Dida to start the shootout. However, Barthez saves Ronaldo, Roberto Carlos & Rivaldo as France prevail on penalties and send the holders out. The lucky charm of Laurent Blanc kissing Fabien Barthez's bald head definitely works!

The other semi-final is a very dull affair. Spain score twice early on through Sanchez Fernando of Real Betis and then shut up shop, managing five shots in the whole game. Switzerland do manage one, but it is off target and Spain go through 2-0.

England have already surpassed their real life counterparts and with Norway to come, it could be a lot worse. They're no pushovers mind, as I found out in that 0-0 draw with them earlier in the season. They've also only conceded once so far, and that was to the hosts. I wish Gazza was available, but Beckham, Dublin & Sheringham are all back in the mix. Incidentally, Gascoigne is the only absentee and he is just a few days away from a return, meaning he could play in the semi-final if we get there. Anyway, it's time.

World Cup Quarter Final – Norway vs England – As it happened

Welcome to Stade Velodrome, the home of Marseille, where Norway and England will do battle for a place in the World Cup semi-finals. This fixture has history – I'm sure you've all heard the 'your boys took one hell of a beating' speech from 1981, when Norway famously beat England. It's much more of an even match these days, as Norway have several Premier League stars on show. Speaking of which, here's the team news.

Team News

One of those stars is out injured for **Norway,** as Tore Andre Flo picked up a twisted ankle in the defeat to France. Dan Eggen is suspended, as is influential midfielder Kenneth Karlsen. Norway's success has been built on a solid defence, with Man Utd's Ronny Johnsen pivotal alongside Liverpool's Bjorn Tore Kvarme. Wimbledon's Stale Solbakken is captain.

Norway: Myhre, Haaland, Kvarme, Johnsen, Bjornebye, Pedersen, Berg, Solbakken (c), Leonhardsen, Bohinen, Neset. **Subs:** Ostenstad, Olsen, E Johnsen, Rekdal, Gill

England welcome back Dion Dublin, David Beckham and Teddy Sheringham from suspension, with the latter having to settle for a place on the bench. Steve McManaman and Rio Ferdinand also drop to the bench.

England: Seaman, G Neville, P Neville, Dublin, Campbell, Adams (c), Beckham, Anderton, Eadie, Scholes, Shearer. **Subs:** Fowler, Sheringham, McManaman, R Ferdinand, Pilkington.

KICK OFF – Let battle commence. Shearer and Scholes kick us off.

5 Minutes – Oyvind Leonhardsen got nine goals for Liverpool last season and he's nearly done it again here. It's a mazy dribble but his final shot is deflected wide. Stian Neset gets his head on the corner but it's wayward.

12 Minutes – Close for England as Campbell meets Beckham's corner but his downward header clips the post. The defender on the line had it covered, but what a chance.

17 Minutes – Shearer is in behind but from a tight angle he blasts the ball a yard wide. More than a half decent chance, that.

23 Minutes – Stian Neset is a handful. The PSV man collects a long ball, turns to try and get a shot away but Tony Adams charges it down.

26 Minutes – **YELLOW CARD**
Alf Inge Haaland of Leeds United is in the book for a deliberate handball, stopping an England attack down the right. Decent position for a free kick too.

27 Minutes – **GOAL FOR ENGLAND! Norway 0 – 1 England (Darren Eadie)**
He's done it again! Eadie justifies his selection and again he's the man in the right place from a corner. Beckham swings in the initial free kick and his good pal Gary Neville is on the end of it, but Thomas Myhre parries it away for a corner. Beckham swings this one in too, Scholes gets the header which hits the bar and there's Darren Eadie to score his second England goal and send the fans delirious.

34 Minutes – England will be delighted to be in front, Norway don't seem like the type of team you want to go behind to.

40 Minutes – We are very short of action. Tiredness or tactical battle? Either way, it suits England.

HALF TIME – Norway 0 – 1 England
Job half done for England, who will already be dreaming of a semi-final clash with Italy or Holland. Norway have yet to have a shot on target, whilst two of England's five shots have troubled Thomas Myhre, but the all-important statistic is that England lead 1-0.

KICK OFF – Norway start the second half, they look fired up. They need to be.

47 Minutes – A Norway corner spells danger for England. Bjornebye's delivery is on the money as always but Stale Solbakken can only head the ball wide. Good chance!

52 Minutes – **YELLOW CARD**
David Beckham is in the book, again. This time a late tackle on Lars Bohinen leaves the referee with no choice but to book the midfield man.

54 Minutes – Norway are pushing hard. Neset is in on goal and looks odds on to score but big Dave Seaman spreads himself well and makes the block.

59 Minutes – Darren Anderton has a pot shot from Scholes' knockdown but it flies over the bar.

66 Minutes – Neset is in again. This time a long ball over the top catches England's back three and the PSV

man is in. Fortunately for England his touch is heavy and Seaman can gather.

72 Minutes – England are twenty minutes away from emulating the squad of Italia 90. Keep your heads!

78 Minutes – **SUBSTITUTION**
Darren Anderton has been quiet tonight, and he is withdrawn for Steve McManaman. A straight swap.

80 Minutes – **YELLOW CARD**
Oyvind Leonhardsen is getting frustrated, as demonstrated here when he ploughs into Sol Campbell. An easier yellow card will never be given.

84 Minutes – Paul Scholes lashes a shot way over the bar. Just keep hold of it!

86 Minutes – **SUBSTITUTION**
Scholes off, Fowler on.An exercise in time wasting.

88 Minutes – OYVIND! England loves you! Ronny Johnsen of all people turns into a right winger, putting the ball in the perfect spot for the arriving Leonhardsen. He must score but instead fluffs his lines and clears the crossbar. Oh my.

89 Minutes – **YELLOW CARD**
Darren Eadie goes in the book for kicking the ball away. Nobody cares.

FULL TIME – Norway 0 – 1 England

England have done it! Darren Eadie's goal has sent them to the World Cup semi-finals and guaranteed at least another two games. England will not want to be in that 3rd/4th place playoff next weekend, that's for certain.

Stale Solbakken takes man of the match, for no obvious reason. It ended up being quite an even game as Norway committed more men forward towards the end, but England just about shaded it.

In the other quarter final, Holland stun Italy 1-0 thanks to Gaston Taument. A headline writers dream, but I'm more than happy with that result given Italy beat us in qualifying, whereas we wiped the floor with Holland in their own back yard, albeit in a friendly.

So the semi-finals are France vs Spain and England vs Holland. To be fair, that's two out of the four real life semi-finalists, so not bad by CM standards.

Gascoigne's bruised jaw has recovered; let's see if he can stay fit for the three days required.

Spain prove to be the party poopers, winning 1-0 in the Stade Velodrome to knock out the hosts. France have fallen short of their real life counterparts, Zidane will never announce himself on the world stage and Spain will have a chance to win their first major tournament 10 years ahead of schedule. Pep Guardiola got the decisive goal, I can't decide if that is ironic or not. Time to nip over to the Stade de France to see if we can join the Spanish, or whether we just have to help

France clean up after their party in the bronze medal playoff.

World Cup Semi Final – Holland vs England – As it happened

Nessun Dorma. Gazza's tears.David Platt's last minute winner. Penalties. Let's do it all again.

I am of course referring to England's run to the Italia 90 Semi-finals, only for that particular dream to be cruelly ended by West Germany on penalties. Stuart Pearce and Chris Waddle wrote themselves into history that night, let's hope the same fate doesn't befall two of the class of '98.

Of course there were some heroes as well as villains for England back in 1990, and this crop of players have plenty to be proud of. The 7-1 win over Denmark will be fondly remembered, as will the comeback win over Chile. It's been a steely England in the knockout stages, but an unlikely hero in Darren Eadie has appeared. Is he the new Gazza? Well, England have the original Gazza back tonight. Let's get some team news.

Team News

We've mentioned England a lot in the intro, but you cannot ignore **Holland**. Playing a revolutionary 3-1-3-3, they've won all five of their matches here in France and are favourites to progress to the final. They are unchanged from their quarter final win over Italy, with no absences.

Holland: Van der Saar, Van Gobbel, Stam, F De Boer, Winter, Jonk, Seedorf, R De Boer, Taument, Overmars,

Kluivert. **Subs:** De Goey, Fraser, Cocu, Bergkamp, Decheiver

For the first time since the tournament began, **England**have a full strength squad to choose from. They opt for just one change, with Gascoigne in for Anderton.
England: Seaman, G Neville, P Neville, Dublin, Campbell, Adams (c), Beckham, Gascoigne, Eadie, Scholes, Shearer. **Subs:** Fowler, Sheringham, Anderton, R Ferdinand, Pilkington.

The anthems are belted out by both sides – this is as big as it gets.

KICK OFF – England kick off, Shearer and Scholes in the centre circle.

4 Minutes – First chance falls for Holland. Aron Winter curls in a corner and Ronald de Boer is first to meet it, but it's loopy and easy for David Seaman. England have looked susceptible from set pieces all tournament

10 Minutes – **GOAL FOR HOLLAND! Holland 1 – 0 England (Gaston Taument)**
The man with the ideal name has scored. Overmars whips in a low cross, Kluivert is first to it and Seaman pulls off a good save to keep it out. The loose ball runs for Taument who makes no mistake from about 10 yards.

16 Minutes – Nearly two! Overmars the architect again, getting a good cross in that Kluivert heads powerfully

towards goal. Seaman has to use every inch of his fingers to tip the ball away for a corner that is easily cleared

20 Minutes – England have had a shot! It's miles away though, Shearer hitting an instinctive shot from way out on the half volley that gets nowhere near the goal.

28 Minutes – **GOAL FOR HOLLAND! Holland 2 – 0 England (Clarence Seedorf)**

Oh dear. It's all gone very wrong very quickly here, as yet another Overmars cross finds Kluivert. Seaman saves yet again, then again from Wim Jonk but the third time from Clarence Seedorf is one too many and that's 2-0. Where are England's defenders!?

33 minutes – Winter crosses the ball into the box and Ronald de Boer rises highest again but once more Seaman saves. The England goalkeeper is overworked.

38 Minutes – Shearer has a shot from slightly closer in this time that is always rising and just clips the bar on the way over.

44 Minutes – England finally test Van der Saar with the last action of the half. Beckham's corner finds Scholes, who hits a low shot that the big Dutchman is more than equal to.

HALF TIME – Holland 2 – 0 England

England's dreams are in tatters. The indignity of a 3rd/4th place playoff beckons again, unless they can turn this around dramatically.

The Dutch have dominated and fully deserve their lead. eight shots, with seven on target, is a great return. England's three with one on target is paltry not only be comparison but in general. Can the second half be any different?

SUBSTITUTION
England have made a half time change, with Teddy Sheringham on for Dion Dublin. It looks like 4-3-3 for England.

KICK OFF – Holland get us back underway, well on their way to a World Cup final.

47 Minutes – **YELLOW CARD**
Ronald de Boer is in the book for a foul on Phil Neville. All very needless really.

48 Minutes – Still the Dutch press. First Kluivert shoots over and then Jonk has a shot blocked by Adams. England can't get out.

52 Minutes – Ronald de Boer gets his head on yet another corner but this time he's off target. The next goal is crucial, and it's almost certainly going to be Holland's at this rate.

57 Minutes – **SUBSTITUTION**

England desperate to get a foothold in the game take off Beckham for Anderton. It could have been any of the front six really.

63 Minutes – The Dutch dominating possession, this is a slow death for England.

69 Minutes – **GOAL FOR ENGLAND! Holland 2 – 1 England (Teddy Sheringham)**
Out of absolutely nothing, England have one back. Half time sub Teddy Sheringham takes aim from 30 yards and the ball bends and swerves it's way past a motionless Van der Saar. It's a great strike, and a potential way back into the match for England.

74 Minutes – Patrick Kluivert could have sealed this on his own. Two chances go begging, both off target. England clinging on.

79 Minutes – **SUBSTITUTION**
Last throw of the dice for England. Robbie Fowler is on for Paul Scholes, who has barely had a kick.

83 Minutes – Still the Dutch can't settle it. Frank de Boer is the latest to fluff his lines, heading yet another corner wide.

87 Minutes – Kluivert to finish it...no! Kluivert goes through one on one with Seaman but shoots wide.

FULL TIME – Holland 2 – 1 England
The dream is over for England. Holland were just too good on the night and England could barely lay a glove

on them. David Seaman takes man of the match after a string of saves, but England were seldom seen as an attacking unit. It'll be a Spain vs Holland final on Sunday.

The third/fourth place playoff is the match nobody wants to be in. On the one hand, it's a reward for a great World Cup but on the other hand, you're knackered and you're playing for a meaningless third place. As a result, I've changed almost the whole eleven and luminaries such as Pilkington, Keown, Southgate and Butt are in the team. Remarkably, given that we are playing the hosts, Owen gives us the lead but France turn it on its head through a Pilkington own goal and a penalty, given away by Pilkington. Maybe that wasn't such a good move anyway. However, we prolong the agony when Gareth Southgate heads home an injury time equaliser meaning we have to go through thirty minutes more of this. That's a nice moment for Southgate though after Euro 96. Maurice scores in extra time to win it on the sudden death rule. Pilkington gets man of the match, which is presumably some sort of sick joke, but it's fourth place for England, just like 1990.

So, the World Cup final is Spain vs Holland. Don't worry, it's not 2010 and Howard Webb isn't involved. Holland win an uninspiring game 1-0 thanks to Aron Winter. On the plus side, it means we were beaten by the hosts. The real life semi-finalists have gone one better and won the whole thing – something they have actually yet to manage having been two time runners up coming into the tournament. Winter lifts the trophy,

and that's it. Japan (sorry South Korea) will host the
2002 World Cup.

So, before I go...

That was the "World According to CM97/98." We've
been through a lot together, hopefully you've found this
stroll down an alternative memory lane to be
enjoyable. We've witnessed some strange things;
Christian Vieri in goal, a Paul Ince hat-trick and Kevin
Pilkington winning the Champions League. But how did
it stack up to the real 1997/98 season?

Arsenal couldn't replicate their double success in
England – Manchester United dominated the league
pretty much from start to finish, whilst Newcastle won
the FA Cup. It turned out to be a memorable treble for
Manchester United, adding the League Cup and
Champions League to their league title. Bolton, Crystal
Palace & Leicester were relegated, which is actually
two out of three with Barnsley taking the plunge in
reality. Sunderland, Middlesbrough & Man City were
promoted. That's quite a change in fortune for Man City,
who were actually relegated. Sunderland suffered a
playoff final defeat to Charlton, meaning
Middlesbrough were the only team to live up their
expectations.

In Spain, Barcelona won the league with a massive
ninety seven points. They managed the same but with
an almost measly seventy four points in the real world.
Athletic Bilbao were their closest challengers that year
with sixty five points, but they were only 14th in the
game, as Real Madrid racked up ninety five points to

145

take 2nd, improving on their 4th place. Looking back, I have no idea how Bilbao managed 2nd. Based on stats alone, their goal difference is only +10 and they had nobody in the top scorer chart. Celta, Mallorca, Merida and Zaragoza were relegated, which is remarkably a perfect score. The game had all four of these teams down to be just as bad as they really were. Barcelona were just pipped to mimicking their Copa del Rey win after losing the final to Atletico Madrid.

Celtic's great comeback will have to wait at least another year, as they sacked Wim Jansen just a couple of months into the season and George Graham was unable to bridge the gap. In the end, Rangers won the title by eighteen points from Celtic to make it ten in a row. The rest of the Scottish season was equally unfamiliar – Livingston, of Division Two, won the Scottish Cup whilst Rangers beat Celtic to win the League cup. Those cups were won by Hearts and Celtic respectively.

Real Madrid came nowhere near replicating their Champions League success, crashing out in the group stages. That allowed Man Utd to win the title for the first time in the "Champions League" era. Chelsea were denied their Cup Winners Cup, with Sparta Prague the unlikely winners instead. Finally, the UEFA Cup final was between two teams from the same country, but rather than Lazio vs Inter we had Bordeaux vs Metz in a far less glamorous affair. Inter's run was ended at their fourth round stage, ironically by another Italian team Udinese, to stop any chance of them repeating the success in game.

I'm pleased to see England's performance under my guidance surpassed that of Glenn Hoddle's men, it was looking pretty worrying when we lost to Italy in qualifying but we got there in the end. Admittedly, the draw opened for us and we didn't really beat any of the major nations on the way to the last four, but we put seven past Denmark and that's got to be worth something. Who would have thought, taking Paul Gascoigne to the tournament turned out better than could have been expected.

With that, the game is all set to run through the retirements and the massive shortlisting process is about to begin. Feel free to find me on Twitter if you want to wish Peter Schmeichel a speedy recover – he'll have a fight on his hands to get his place back though, Kevin Pilkington's earned a new contract!

I hope you enjoyed this book from The Higher Tempo Press. If you did, please leave a review on whichever platform you purchased it from.

To get more books from The Higher Tempo Press visit www.thehighertempopress.com

Don't forget to go and buy the "Johnny Cooper, Championship Manager" series is now available from the same shop!

JOHNNY COOPER, CHAMPIONSHIP MANAGER
The Second Season Syndrome
(according to Championship Manager)

Chris Darwen